the LEADER'S CALL

4 INSIGHTS for LEADING YOURSELF at the NEXT LEVEL

Grace Owen

o g
publishing

This book is dedicated to my mother,
Rose Abena Owusua Mintah
1943-2010

og publishing
A division of Grace Owen Solutions Ltd

A CIP catalogue record for this book is available from the British Library.

ISBN 978-0-9563908-4-4

Editorial team: Leda Sammarco and Jane Collinson

Design by Julia Lloyd Photography by Jake Green

Printed and bound by CPI Group (UK) Ltd, Croydon, CR0 4YY

2 4 6 8 10 9 7 5 3 1

CONTENTS

ACKNOWLEDGEMENTS

To my husband Simon for his unconditional love, shoulder massages and endless cups of tea. To my son Ben for the latest football news and big hugs. To my sister Rose Coleman for your encouragement and support. To Ashley, Claudine, Hannah and Jorja Matthews for all the socialising. To Alex Ntung, Josie Hai Diep, Mebrak Ghebreweldi and Penny Berry for their time and 'fresh' pairs of eyes! Thanks to everyone who kept asking 'is it finished yet?'. To the leaders I have met over the past twenty something years...it was a pleasure! To my wonderful publishing and promotions team – it was fun to do this a second time – Leda Sammarco, Jane Collinson, Julia Lloyd, Karin Jones, Susan Moore and Caren Johnstone. To readers of The Leader's Call, I have written this book to be a source of practical inspiration. May it be just what you are looking for...enjoy!

INTRODUCTION

MY STORY...

It was a warm, humid day in May 2012 and while travelling in a taxi I noticed the new road, which during my trip the year before had been incomplete. I was visiting Accra the capital of Ghana in West Africa and, strangely, seeing the road inspired me. This concrete infrastructure, a symbol of connectivity and progress, was an example of the change being reported excitedly across Africa. Then it happened...I felt the inner urge.

'What was that?' I wondered. For a split second I imagined being part of the modern developments in Ghana, my homeland. A jumble of questions came. How could I make a contribution to this country or even the continent of Africa? What did I have to offer? What did this feeling mean? Intuitively, I knew it was an important moment.

I named this inner urge *The Leader's Call*. It described what I had felt in that moment: an impulse combining ambition, excitement, desire, adventure and possibility. On my return to London *The Leader's Call* took me on a 'heart-lurching' and at times 'mind-twisting' exploration during which I sought to answer the questions raised by the inner urge. After two years, I came to a conclusion. The inner urge was moving me to the next level of my leadership experience...I was in transition, again. For me, this meant being a leader who was committed to and active in making the world a better place. It meant redirecting my time, energy, personality, values, talents, experience, skills, knowledge, resources and network. It took another year to achieve that reality.

The Leader's Call changed my life, not abruptly or drastically but slowly and deliberately. In fact, I now know that I had been responding to it subconsciously for nearly four decades, but in May 2012 I felt the inner urge very powerfully and 'heard' that call to action as if for the first time. Why? It may be due to what had happened on Easter Monday a few weeks before.

My family and I had a near death experience. Our car crashed on a motorway in the UK. Despite crossing three lanes of traffic and hitting two trees on the verge, we emerged from the wreckage with only cuts, bruising and in shock. It was, to us, a miraculous escape.

It was a life-changing event that led me to re-evaluate my life and work. I became more sensitised to my inner yearnings, as I was when I felt the inner urge on that new road in Accra. Your own hearing of *The Leader's Call* may not come as the result of a dramatic event like mine, or it may be even more so. However, at some point in your life and for a reason that is unique to you, you will hear *The Leader's Call*.

It has taken me a few years to consolidate, clarify and conclude my response to this inner urge. Why? How? All shall become clear as you read this book!

The inner urge gave me the conviction to stop leading

in places and ways that I was used to, comfortable with and that mainly brought material reward. It took me across many invisible thresholds of growth as I bravely went to places I had not been to before. It revealed a deep motivation that I had held since childhood – a desire to make a difference to others.

Looking back, I can see that my experience of leadership began in childhood. Aged nine, I was invited to become captain of the primary school's netball team. A teacher spotted the leadership potential in me and nurtured it. In that role I had to participate and cooperate with, encourage and guide my peers. Together we celebrated success and learned to improve our game through failure. Since then I have experienced the highs, lows and plateaus that come with the leadership territory, navigating from one level to the next.

As a teenager I was coordinator of a small church music group. I 'fell' into this role simply because I was passionate about playing the guitar! I embraced this responsibility and enjoyed developing my musical skills. However, being shy I struggled with the visibility and exposure that performing to an audience brought. It took years to get used to this, but during that time I discovered my talent for planning and organising. I had a natural ability to see details while appreciating and understanding that there was also a bigger picture.

As a young adult, after completing university, I became a team leader as part of the graduate management training programme with Marks and Spencer. My biggest challenge here was communicating effectively with people of different ages and cultures. I overcame this by learning to listen (trying not to think about what I would say next), by asking questions and building relationships that were professional and personal. I found that most people loved to talk about their lives and families. Developing this interpersonal skill over time raised my self-esteem and self-confidence.

My repertoire of leadership skills was put to the biggest test when I was appointed head of learning and development for Costa Coffee. This role brought new dimensions such as leading and developing a national team, directing the innovation of an organisation learning strategy and then leading a group to implement it. Being so busy meant that my work-life balance really suffered. At the end of this assignment I was nearly burnt out.

Up until then, I had been a leader in organisations where the next level meant a promotion. I had stayed in environments where I was familiar with the ebb and flow of corporate life. That changed in 2003, when I moved out of the comfort zone of employment to start a niche business. Beforehand, my primary focus had been leading others, now I was solely responsible for leading myself!

Developing the business required me to hone my skills and develop new ones, so that I could offer appropriate, effective services and products to my clients. These included coaching, writing, marketing, consulting, training, facilitating, mentoring, speaking, teaching and advising. Each of these took me up to a new level within my business and myself.

At this point my leadership story represents major shifts from one level of leadership to the next in a way that was typical, even the norm within a conventional work environment. The leadership responsibilities, skills and experience were increasing gradually and I had pretty much expected that. However, the next level does not always mean that you progress up an organisation chart. The status and title that comes with a more senior position is not as important as what you are being called to and the ways in which you are required to use your unique abilities. Being a leader is a big responsibility wherever you are.

When I was invited to chair a new local community youth project and become a trustee of a new non-governmental organisation (NGO), these next levels of leadership presented unexpected opportunities. I was supporting grass roots organisations with a handful of people who did not have a global profile or easy access to resources. I extended my research and writing skills in these roles: writing strategic papers and reports, monthly newsletters for supporters and copy for websites.

For years, I had held an ambition to write a trilogy of self-help development books but I did not know that this was a next level. Writing my first book *The Career Itch – 4 Steps for Taking Control of What You Do Next* was a new experience and an act of leadership. No one else (that I knew of at the time) had written a book about the inner restlessness that many of us have around the direction of our careers. Since then I have supported five other first-time authors to turn their experiences into books that inspire and inform.

I can see that hearing and acting upon *The Leader's Call* has taken me to unexpected places. Being responsible for coordinating a team of cooks at a homeless shelter had not been on my radar. Nor was my being identified as one of a hundred African Diaspora ChangeMakers in the UK. I did not know that I would become a non-executive director for Camfed International, develop Pan-African leaders in West, North, East and South Africa or become founder and director of community legacy project, African Diaspora Kids.

All of this because of *The Leader's Call!*

My response to *The Leader's Call* in May 2012 shows up in my life each day, in three ways.

1. **I am developing leaders** who want to make a difference to others from their virtual, open-plan and mobile offices, from their homes and schools, from high street cafés and inner-city places of worship – in fact from wherever they happen to be.

2. **I am a philanthropist** who supports causes that are making Africa a better place through nurturing and releasing the leadership potential of women, men and children on the continent and in the Diaspora.

3. **I am a writer** whose books encourage, equip and empower readers to take responsibility for their personal and professional selves so that they excel. They in turn enable others at home, in teams, organisations, communities and society to flourish.

My story demonstrates that you can come to leadership through a variety of means. It may be an invitation because someone has spotted potential in you. You might take on a leadership role and discover you enjoy it! Perhaps, for whatever reason, you find it stressful so you want to give up or indeed, keep on trying! Opportunities will keep coming your way whether you feel ready or not. I believe leaders are born and made.

It does not matter whether you are just starting out on the leadership journey or beginning another chapter of your leadership story after years of experience. The next level is not about getting an ego boost or becoming a guru. Instead *The Leader's Call* is a signal that it is time to move to different places and spaces inside yourself and out in the world. It reflects the leader you have been, who you are now and who you are ready to become.

The leaders I have worked with, in the past and present, have felt the inner urge but like me they did not have a name for it. What I noticed, when looking back on my own leadership transitions and at what these other leaders were telling me, is that this inner urge always precedes the next level. Identifying and naming this feeling, and wanting to inspire and guide other leaders, is what led me to write this book.

These are leaders from all walks of life, with a title and without, with a remit and without, with a profile and without. They are natural leaders and self-taught leaders. They are early developers and late bloomers. They are leaders that 'sink' and 'swim' at the next level, they succeed and fail – publicly and privately. Some leaders have access to resources, others have little but they are driven to keep on keeping on. These leaders are found in every profession, they are generalists, specialists or experts in their field.

When these leaders respond to *The Leader's Call* they move, not always willingly, happily, smoothly or consciously, to the next level of their leadership experience.

Are you feeling the inner urge? Have you heard *The Leader's Call*? Whether your answer is 'yes', 'I'm not sure' or 'not yet', I have written this book for you. I believe that leaders are change makers and game changers. The world needs you!

This book distils the countless interactions, observations and conversations I have had with leaders. It describes what I have noticed and sensed. It defines what makes leaders excel and derail. *The Leader's Call* impels you to action: whether you are a natural-born leader or whether you have nurtured and honed your leadership abilities over time.

Now that you know my leadership story, I would like to know about yours. I wonder what led you to pick up this book and what leadership responsibilities, skills and experiences have brought you to where you are right now.

YOUR LEADERSHIP STORY

Take this short self-assessment and circle one letter in each category that, overall, best represents your leadership experiences to date.

1 How did you come to leadership?
a) By surprise
b) Through an opportunity
c) Career progression
d) It's in your nature

2 Which of these words best describes how you feel about being a leader?
a) Resistant
b) Interested
c) Challenged
d) Willing

3 What concerns do you have about leading?

    a) I'd rather not be a leader

    b) I'm not sure if I am doing it right

    c) I'd like to be more consistent

    d) I might miss out on an opportunity

4 How do you spend most of your time?

    a) Trying to stay motivated

    b) Getting things done on my to-do list

    c) Directing others to get things done

    d) Exploring how best to make things happen

5 What advice would you give a new leader?

    a) Don't do it

    b) Keep going

    c) You will improve

    d) Learn from everything

6 What do you need right now?

    a) Someone to guide me

    b) More experience

    c) To balance life and work

    d) Reflection time

7 How would you describe your next level of leadership?

    a) Staying where I am

    b) Leading a team, group or project

    c) Leading in the community or society

    d) Leading wherever I go

Interpreting your responses

There are four leadership types that are likely to reflect your leadership story to date.

Mostly a = reluctant leader

Mostly b = new leader

Mostly c = experienced leader

Mostly d = mentor leader

Have a look at the table on pages 16–17 to read more about your leadership type and what you can do about it.

These types of leader are drawn from my own experiences of being a leader, of leading teams and of developing leadership in others. They are the stories of leaders I have met, worked with, researched, listened to and read about. These are not the only types that reflect where you might have been, where you are or where you might end up as you move to the next level. However, these are the recurring stories and dominant narratives that emerge when leaders talk openly and honestly about their experiences.

It is really important that you do not judge one type of leader as better or worse than another. We are all a combination of these leaders depending on the places where we lead now and where we may lead next. What these types demonstrate is that being a leader is not easy or straightforward. This is partly due to the nature of the different arenas in which leaders are required to operate. I call these the five domains, and each one involves its own challenges.

MOSTLY A
Reluctant leader

Situation You're not sure that you are a leader and perceive this part of your role as a task you don't want. Your resistance to leadership is making you unhappy, fearful and vulnerable. You can't understand why others trust you and want to give you more responsibility.

Cause You have a lot of unexplored judgements and assumptions about what it means to be a leader, about leading and leadership.

Risk If you continue to be ambivalent you may underperform, become defensive and lose the trust that others have put in you.

Opportunity Are you willing to challenge your judgements and assumptions about what being a leader, leading and leadership is and can be? You may be inspired by what you discover!

What to do Go online or to your local bookshop and browse what is available. Acquire 3 resources:
1. the autobiography of a leader you respect
2. a book about the skills needed for leading well
3. a resource that shows and explains the wide variety of leadership models and styles.

MOSTLY B
New leader

Situation You accept that you're a leader and you are proud of the fact. You have worked hard to reach this point. You are like a sponge soaking up everything around you. You deliver at 100% and are willing to sacrifice yourself if it means you gain more responsibility.

Cause Others spotted your potential and you fought to reach this level. Deep down you believe that you were born to lead.

Risk Rapid movement to the next level doesn't equal an effective leader. What lessons are you missing in your race to progress?

Opportunity Reflect on what you are doing well, what you are not doing well and what needs improvement. An honest self-review will enable you to become aware of strengths and growth areas.

What to do Once you've completed the self-review ask three leaders that you know, trust and respect to give you their honest opinion too. They will confirm and challenge your self-perception, helping you to identify character qualities and blind spots. Listen openly and thank them for their perceptions.

MOSTLY C
Experienced leader

Situation You've been a leader for years and moved through many next levels of leadership. You have learned through trial, error and from other leaders about what is required to create the conditions where others perform at their best. Often you've felt burdened by too much responsibility.

Cause You have realised that being a leader is less about doing the tasks and more about developing others to do the tasks.

Risk Staying at a level that is familiar and where you know what is expected of you. Be alert to change, it is coming very soon.

Opportunity Take a moment to write your leadership timeline, noting the major and minor shifts from one level to the next. What common themes are there? What might derail your proven track record?

What to do Find a coach and/or mentor and/or a group of peers who will support and challenge you to extract as much learning from all the experiences you've had to date. Then start to prepare for the next level of leadership armed with renewed self-awareness, self-knowledge and self-confidence.

MOSTLY D
Mentor leader

Situation You've been the reluctant leader, new leader and experienced leader. You've moved to the next level on more occasions than you realise. Leaders are drawn to your warmth, openness, and experience. They're inspired by your humanity, knowledge and clarity.

Cause You are still learning how to model vulnerability and strength. You believe that mentees are teaching you too.

Risk Thinking that you are doing all you can. There are more leaders who need to hear your voice...where are they?

Opportunity To reflect more deeply on your leadership practice. To assess what 'work' there is still to do on yourself. You know that perfection is impossible, you just want to keep learning.

What to do Make a record of your leadership experiences using conversation, writing, metaphor or all three. Use this 'body of work' to identify and share the key nuggets of wisdom and encouragement that you want to pass on to your mentees and the leaders that you haven't met yet.

THE FIVE DOMAINS

DOMAIN 1

Leading yourself – your inner world of feelings, thoughts and outer world of behaviour and experiences

DOMAIN 2

Leading others – in the family, groups, teams

DOMAIN 3

Leading functions – departments, ministries, directorates, business units

DOMAIN 4

Leading organisations – corporations, institutions, associations, industries

DOMAIN 5

Leading in society – communities, villages, cities, districts, regions, countries, nations

These domains are subject to uncontrollable conditions, diverse cultures, competing demands and resource constraints. All of this amounts to change – constant change that evolves rapidly and arises from a multiplicity of external and internal factors, from people power to economics, restructures to technological advances.

Sit in a meeting, open a newspaper, speak to a colleague on another continent, listen to the news, watch

TV or search online. The conversations, in the main, are about change: what has happened to our financial systems, what is happening to the Earth's climate and what will happen in the war on terror? Change is what makes the domains a harsh environment because they lack certainty, stability and continuity, but at the same time change is needed.

Change is disruptive. At best it ushers in new ways of doing things, it generates diverse perspectives and leads to innovations and improvements. Leaders learn new skills, adjust their behaviour and develop tenacity. They test alternatives for doing what needs to be done; nothing stands still and they persevere. Whether we create, adapt to or resist change it keeps us on our mental, emotional and physical toes. Leading in these domains can make any leader feel insecure, powerless and vulnerable. It is important to remember that although we do have control over some things there are many more that we do not. How can you cope with this?

You could choose an inspirational quotation or a poem and put this on your desk or wall. Some leaders have favourite mottos and sayings that encourage them as they go into and through the leadership labyrinth. Either way, some form of visible inspiration will help you to deal with the inevitable challenges and frustrations that being a leader brings.

I find The Serenity Prayer very useful for grounding and anchoring me when change seems insurmountable and difficult.

'God, grant me the serenity to accept
the things I cannot change,
courage to change the things I can and
wisdom to know the difference'

Reinhold Niebuhr, Theologian

When I ponder on my leadership experiences I see that I
have led and am leading in all five of these interconnected
domains. I am a leader, parent, business owner, service
provider and active citizen. I have criss-crossed the
permeable and invisible boundaries of the five domains.

Think about your own leadership experiences.

Into which of these domains has *The Leader's Call*
moved you over the years? Where are you now? Where
are you going to next?

THE FIVE DOMAINS OF LEADERSHIP

HOW CAN LEADERS EXCEL IN THE FIVE DOMAINS?

At the nub of any leader's success is leading themselves because wherever they practise leadership, they are the common denominator. Is it possible to lead others at the next level and beyond if we cannot lead ourselves? No! In the past, leaders said 'do as I say, not as I do'. In the twenty-first century it is an unacceptable mantra and with the pervasive, growing scrutiny of leaders in every sector, industry and profession, it is not a wise mode of thought or action.

If leaders always tell people what to do instead of showing them how to do it, they lack integrity and will quickly lose the respect and trust of their followers. Better to say 'I am seeking to "walk my talk" as best as possible, let me know when I am not and forgive me when I fail.' Every leader is a work in progress and so is every follower.

In this book I offer four insights for leading yourself at the next level so that you can seek to be and do your best wherever you are. I use the acronym CALL to articulate these insights.

- **Insight 1** C is for Commitment – moving to the next level
- **Insight 2** A is for Authenticity –becoming who you are
- **Insight 3** L is for Learning – developing mastery
- **Insight 4** L is for Legacy – sustaining your contribution

We will look more closely at the four insights later in this book; for now it is important that you know what they are. These insights will not turn you into a perfect leader. As I observed earlier, the context of the leader's domain makes this impossible; plus being human means our flaws, foibles and flunks will inevitably show up.

We can still aspire to high standards and excellence. If you do struggle, be kind, forgiving and accepting of your imperfections because you are bound to make mistakes.

The purpose of this book is to equip you as a leader to become more conscious, confident, competent and consistent. I believe these are at the heart of being an effective leader and, I also hope, that they are the ambition of every leader.

Leading ourselves at the next level is our responsibility. As leaders, if we use our power boldly, deepen our self-awareness, expand our self-knowledge and take care of ourselves all while responding to *The Leader's Call*, we will be true role models for leaders, followers and all those we interact with.

MOVING ON

Now that you know more about me, have revisited your own leadership story, read about the five domains and been introduced to the four insights, I wonder how you are feeling.

The Leader's Call signals that you are in transition, moving 'up a gear', or perhaps it is telling you that you have just arrived. Before we look at the four insights in greater detail there is much more to say about *The Leader's Call*.

Shall we go?

THE LEADER'S CALL

> 'Principled and visionary leaders are
> still too few in number'
> Wangari Matthai

WHAT IS THE LEADER'S CALL?

In a nutshell it is an inner urge that moves you to the next level of your leadership experience.

The Leader's Call is like an internal pressure cooker, it builds up over time until you 'release the steam' by taking action so that you can move to the next level, whether this is your first or tenth experience of such an urge. *The Call* attracts your attention to announce a new opportunity, which might be of niche proportions or even take you onto the global stage.

You are being called to lead in one or more of the five domains of leadership.

When you lead in these domains, you are giving time while bringing your energy, personality, values, talents, experience, skills, knowledge, resources and network to make a difference to situations, projects and other people.

In taking on a new set of challenges you will be put to the test. At times it will feel very difficult, to the extent that you may want to give up. Completing the next level successfully means staying committed to what you are there to do, being true to yourself, learning as you go and being aware of what you are creating in the long term. You will acquire so much more than you might have imagined. There will be pitfalls along the way and your character blind spots will be exposed. However, if you are willing to learn through these, and continue playing to your strengths, then you will grow personally, professionally and be ready to move to the next level when *The Leader's Call* sounds.

THE FIVE DOMAINS OF LEADERSHIP

WHAT WILL HAPPEN AT THE NEXT LEVEL?

Your next leadership experience may feel slightly familiar or take you right out of your comfort zone. It might be possible to complete this in your spare time or on a part or full-time basis. You may already be in the domain or are on your way to it.

When the inner urge is present, there is a new leadership opportunity waiting that is YOU-shaped. This means the next level needs your unique talents, personality, motivation, experience, values and perspective. During it you will unveil more of your authentic self.

What will happen at the next level? It could range from doing something you believe in and are ready to take a stand for. You may feel ready to help others develop themselves. Reading this book means that your self-belief is greater than before, even if it does not feel that way. You want to become the best leader you can be. Right now you have the courage to lead yourself – the inner leader is creating and recreating the outer leader.

The Leader's Call will generate a host of questions in your mind that mostly begin with Why? What? When? Who? Where? How? As you move forward you will discover the answers to these questions. Do not be overwhelmed by them. They are designed to help not hinder you as you navigate the new spaces and places you are going to.

Remember that *The Leader's Call* is a symptom and not the cause of how you are feeling, which is probably a combination of nervous and excited. *The Leader's Call* is simply a reminder and invitation to step up and move to the next level.

My leadership story reveals that even at a young age *The Leader's Call* was there. It beckons children, teenagers and adults. You are never too young or too old to hear it. It is for ordinary people who aspire to do extraordinary things. It will make its presence known multiple times throughout your leadership journey.

Here are five don'ts and dos to remember when hearing *The Leader's Call*.

Don't ✗	Do ✓
• Ignore it because you think something is wrong	• Welcome it
• Suppress and deny it	• Acknowledge how you feel (at the very least to yourself)
• Think it will go away	• Get excited about it
• Be overwhelmed or afraid of it	• Share its arrival with a loved one
• Try to get rid of it	• Read this book from cover to cover!

LEADERSHIP CAN BE A BIG ASK

How do you know if you are hearing *The Leader's Call*? On page 27 is a list of eighteen questions that leaders I have worked with repeatedly ask me. I have grouped these questions into those that relate to the inner or outer world of a leader.

Tick all the questions that apply to you.

Inner world

○ Why am I feeling like this?

○ Do I have what it takes to be a leader?

○ What is the next level of leadership for me?

○ Why are people always asking me to lead?

○ How do I respond to this feeling?

○ What choices do I need to make?

○ Who will I become?

○ Why does that leader inspire me so much?

○ Am I ready to move to the next level of leadership?

Outer world

○ What is my contribution to the world?

○ Who are the people for whom I can make a difference?

○ Where should I be making a difference?

○ What resources will I need?

○ How can I meet someone else's needs?

○ What are my measures of success?

○ Will I need to retrain?

○ What's the plan of action?

○ How will I know I've reached the destination?

How many questions did you tick? . . . .

(write the number here)

If you suspect that you are hearing *The Leader's Call* and have asked three or more of these inner and outer world questions then the time has come to go on a soulful quest to discover what the next level of leadership is for you.

HOW URGENT DOES IT FEEL?

Feeling the inner urge is like hearing a voice that says, 'Go to the next level of your leadership, start the next chapter, take up the challenge, it's a new season, seize the opportunity, begin this phase, establish another milestone.' The inner urge is what enables you to fulfil your greatest leadership potential. This voice can be quiet, noticeable or loud. The pressure you feel can be minimal or significant.

Use the call-o-meter (opposite) to rate the urgency of your call. Do not think about it too much or try to be exact; trust your gut instinct. What is important is that you have a general idea; the rest will emerge as you start taking action. Mark your position on the call-o-meter by making a note on the diagram or elsewhere for future reference.

The call-o-meter enables you to see clearly the extent of your feelings about your leadership call so that you can openly acknowledge them. What else are you feeling?

Remember that being a leader means you will always hear *The Leader's Call*. It is the driving force of your leadership experience. It helps develop your leadership abilities. It takes you to the next leadership challenge. It reminds you to stay committed, to be authentic, to keep learning and sustain your leadership contribution.

The wonderful thing about the call is that it will get quieter when you have taken up your leadership

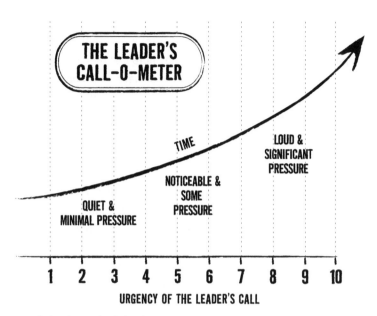

THE LEADER'S CALL-O-METER

TIME

QUIET & MINIMAL PRESSURE

NOTICEABLE & SOME PRESSURE

LOUD & SIGNIFICANT PRESSURE

1 2 3 4 5 6 7 8 9 10

URGENCY OF THE LEADER'S CALL

1-4 quiet and minimal pressure
4-7 noticeable and some pressure
7+ loud and significant pressure

opportunity and louder when you haven't. In other words, it will be less intense or more intense depending on whether you are close to or far away from the place you are moving to next. So, keep noticing what you are feeling!

Many of us have been told not to trust our feelings because, according to some, they make us too emotional, uncontrollable or childish. Many of us, including me, have grown up in families, cultures and societies that tell us to supress how we really feel. Today, we know that 'keeping a lid' on our feelings can make us deeply unhappy, difficult to be around and affect our wellbeing or performance in detrimental ways.

Our range of emotions is important because they are part of what make us human. They help us when we are trying to make sense of a situation or person. Do not shut your emotions away, suppress them or pretend you are not feeling anything when you are. When it comes to *The Leader's Call*, staying in touch with how you feel is vital. If you are unable to identify the inner urge, you can miss a wonderful opportunity and others will miss your unique presence and value. This is your gift to the world.

The fact I was in Ghana when I heard the call has turned out to be significant because I am now making a difference to women, men and children in Africa and the Diaspora. Where were you when you felt the inner urge? When did you hear *The Leader's Call*?

BENEFITS ALL ROUND

Responding to *The Leader's Call*, will change how you use your time and where your energy goes. It will help you to be focused so that you maximise these precious and limited resources. Moving to the next level might sound like you are doing all the giving. I have been amazed at just how much I have received in return! Here are ten significant things I have gained as I have moved to my next levels of leadership.

- *Lifelong friendships and an expanded network*
- *Working with a variety of people*
- *Confidence to set clearer boundaries*
- *Ability to take calculated risks*
- *A deeper understanding of being a leader and what leadership means*

- *Cultural insight from travelling to different places*
- *Resilience from dealing with setbacks*
- *Discovering ways to access new resources*
- *A 'platform' for influencing systemic change*
- *Insights that I can share with other leaders!*

Which of the things on my list would you like to acquire? What other benefits do you have in mind?

LEADING YOURSELF THROUGH THIS BOOK

Working through this book is like having a personal leadership development consultation with me. It will require you to engage in inner enquiry and take outer action. I will share parts of my leadership story and the stories of other leaders who have been where you are and where you are going to. Be encouraged. You are not alone.

Here are some tips to help you get the most out of this book.

- *Work in sequence through the four CALL insights – Commitment, Authenticity, Learning and Legacy. Allow plenty of time to complete each one thoroughly, before working on the next insight. Each one relates to the next level and how to navigate it while you are there. If you come across something that does not resonate with you, then keep an open mind. It may highlight an area of potential growth for you.*

- *Each insight is interspersed with questions for reflection. Do not be tempted to skip the 'actions to take', as they are an important part of the whole process. If you have difficulty with any of them, take a break or discuss it with someone who knows you well and whose opinion you trust. Consider setting yourself a target of completing one insight per week or month. Imagine you are completing a You-shaped development programme.*

- *Make notes as you go along. I write in all the self-help books I read because to me they are study guides. Return to your notes and see what patterns have emerged. Alternatively, treat yourself to a gorgeous journal to record your ideas and your own insights!*

- *Read the book with a positive intention and be curious. This will help you to become aware of the next level and bring clarity about where you are moving to next.*

The Leader's Call is about the process as much as the outcome. As I have explained it will appear throughout your leadership experience; it is not a one-off. Reading this book may help you to discover your biggest ambition or deepest purpose (and if so, that is wonderful), but you may simply move to the next level of leadership and enjoy it more!

When I first noticed *The Leader's Call*, I was unsure *and* excited as I suspect you are too. Having spent so much time with other leaders, I believe that there are a multitude of us who are experiencing the inner urge. *The Leader's Call* is a universal human experience that all leaders will notice at some point as their leadership story unfolds.

Since you are reading this book I have assumed that you are ready to take action. You may want to read this book with other leaders and work through each section together.

This is a great way to keep the momentum going and finish the book. You may also want to share what you discover by writing it down or discussing with a mentor or your nearest and dearest.

WHERE NEXT?

It is your choice whether to dip your toe into this learning experience or dive into the deep end! The more willing you are, the deeper you go and the greater your chances of a professional and personal transformation.

Each of the four insights is a signpost that marks your progress. Self-help can feel lonely and difficult, so wherever you are moving to next, my role is to be your leadership mentor and coach. I will help you discover your own insights and share mine. I want the best for you because you deserve it and the world is waiting for you to step up and step out. I will support and challenge you along the way.

Sign the personal declaration on the next page as a demonstration of your willingness to do what it takes to complete this book. Doing this is an act of courage and one of many actions to come.

I . . . . (insert name)
am READY and WILLING to READ
THE LEADER'S CALL
and COMPLETE the FOUR INSIGHTS for
LEADING MYSELF at THE NEXT LEVEL

signed . . . .
date . . . .

Let's go...

'It is by coming and going that the bird builds its nest'
Ghanaian proverb

INSIGHT

C
is for
COMMITMENT

> 'The irony of commitment is that
> it's deeply liberating'
>
> Anne Morris

MOVING TO THE NEXT LEVEL

Perhaps you are thinking, 'Grace, it's so obvious to include commitment as one of the four insights for leading yourself at the next level.' My reply would be, 'I agree with you!' However, I am curious to understand why leaders (like you, me and others) find it so hard to give and keep commitment as we move to the next level and take up our new assignments, especially when we are doing something that has purpose and meaning.

As a leader, I have moved from one position to another. I am responsible for making things happen. I know too that making things happen requires persistent commitment!

So... Why is it easier to procrastinate?

Well, because it is easy to put off what we cannot 'get hold of' immediately or what we cannot appreciate fully even if we feel a powerful urge towards it. Deep down we sense that the next level is asking more of us, and the pending 'weight of responsibility' is too great, hence the inner resistance. We move away, not towards it.

Why does it feel like a wrench as we let go of one thing and start another?

We all struggle with endings and new beginnings. What we know feels safe and the unknown can be intimidating. Whether the next level is vaguely familiar or brand new you may still be wondering (and trying to work out) what you are letting yourself in for.

Hearing *The Leader's Call* means that one or more opportunities from the five domains are calling you forth. Whether you are a new or an experienced leader you are likely to feel cautious and reticent at the thought of moving on.

Making a commitment to this next level is powerful. It is the catalyst, which turns possibilities into reality. It is the bridge between where you are now and where you are going. It is the key that opens a door to a whole new adventure. Giving your commitment means that the time has come to make a greater impact, to fulfil your potential and purpose elsewhere rather than staying in your comfort zone.

I am certainly not suggesting that leaders should take on lots more commitments; they usually have more than enough to do already. On the contrary, I am interested in enabling leaders to be more committed by discerning what is most important at the next level and which opportunity (or opportunities) is right for them.

In this chapter we will reflect on our definition of commitment and see how leaders relate to it. We will explore common obstacles and how to overcome them. I will share my experience of making and keeping commitment. Throughout the chapter there are actions for you to take in order to draw out and develop further your understanding of this insight. All this is designed to empower you, when you hear *The Leader's Call*, to move on to the next level and see it through to completion.

WHAT IS THIS THING CALLED COMMITMENT?

What springs to mind when you read the word commitment? If you think it is a 'serious' word it might automatically make you feel nervous, burdened or even jog memories of a time when you took responsibility for a task you did not want to do. You may recall a past relationship and remember when a more personal commitment was discussed.

The word commitment may have a more positive connotation because as a risk taker you are not afraid to dream and do, or boldly go where few venture. You have learned that commitment brings inspiring responsibilities not just difficult ones. Perhaps you are relishing the next level, whatever it brings to you personally and professionally!

What thoughts and feelings are you experiencing?

Commitment is a word so overused that it has become heavily loaded with assumption and expectation. Add to this our personal values and beliefs, and we can get hung up by this word, unable to see it in a new light or bring a different perspective to it. While I do have an opinion, I do not believe there is one right, absolute and single definition of commitment. Before we go on, it is important for **you** to define what it means to you now.

Moving to and through many new levels of leadership experience has taught me the value of writing things down. Why? First, we all have a lot going on in our minds, so we need to get out of our heads as much as possible! Second, there is a big difference between what I think about a word and what it means to me when I write it down. Writing something down can often reveal things we were not aware of previously.

Take a few minutes to ask yourself: What does commitment mean to me at this moment in time?

You may answer with a specific word such as promise or responsibility. Or you may get a feeling of expansion or restriction. Trust what shows up for you and write down your answer.

Now, think about your personal and professional life.

How do you identify and prioritise these commitments? Is your professional life more important than your personal life?

If your answer is 'yes', 'no' or 'I'm not sure', consider why that might be.

Next work through the activity on page 41. I have included an example of my answers to the questions to guide you.

Revisit your answers to amend and add to them as we go through this chapter.

Many of us are used to thinking about commitment as a vow, contract or obligation which suggests legality, imposed structures and a rigid framework. That is how I defined it too. However, over time, commitment has come to be, for me, more about dedication, persistence and loyalty. These are qualities that leaders seek to embody as they encounter ambiguity, dilemmas and upheaval in the five domains where leadership happens. In order to flourish you will need to be adaptable and spontaneous.

COMMITMENT IS...
Grace's example

1. Choose one personal or professional example of a commitment.
Being a parent to my son through the fun, difficult and everyday times.

2. How do you feel about this?
I feel excited, daunted, joyful, challenged and privileged.

3. What metaphor best describes this commitment?
The nurturing of an oak sapling – growing a young slender tree into an older strong one.

4. Describe the colour/s that represents this commitment.
Colours of the rainbow, red, orange, yellow, green, blue, indigo and violet. This spectrum depicts the range of different situations that a parent will deal with.

5. What smell do you associate with this commitment?
The scent of a well-known deodorant/body spray which he received for Christmas! He was so excited about it and somehow it marked a shift from child to young man.

6. Define what commitment is to you (based on your example).
Taking my responsibility seriously. Being aware of the multitude of emotions that I relate to it and how these drive my behaviour. Noticing the impact of my interaction and staying flexible. Being, doing and saying my best and admitting when I get it wrong.

Now it is your turn!

COMMITMENT IS...

1. Choose one personal or professional example of a commitment.

   ....

   ....

2. How do you feel about this?

   ....

   ....

3. What metaphor best describes this commitment?

   ....

   ....

4. Describe the colour/s that represents this commitment.

   ....

   ....

5. What smell do you associate with this commitment?

   ....

   ....

6. Define what commitment is to you (based on your example).

   ....

   ....

GRACE'S COMMITMENTS

Short-term commitments e.g. moments, hours, days

- *Signing an online petition to support a cause that I care about*
- *Making a donation to a friend's fundraising campaign*
- *Agreeing to write a character reference for a leader I have worked with*
- *Meeting a senior leader to discuss personal development and succession plans*
- *Going on a one-day retreat to review and reflect on my life and leadership roles*

Medium-term commitments e.g. weeks, months, seasons

- *Preparing to lead the study group that meets at my home*
- *Designing the prototype of a client's leadership development solution*
- *Abstaining from sweet treats and alcohol for the Spring*
- *Facilitating the first of four Reflective Practice sessions for senior leaders*
- *Quarterly meeting with collaborators to further our joint project*

Long-term commitments e.g. years, life, after death

- *Annual updates with my virtual team to discuss business performance and planning*
- *Strategic review with the entrepreneur I've worked with for over five years*
- *Visiting local secondary schools with my husband to find the best fit for our son*
- *Discussing book promotion with my PR agent*
- *Amending my living will to include my latest wishes*

What does commitment look like in practice?

Commitment may be when you impulsively sign a petition at your front door or online to show your support for a campaign that expresses your worldview. It might be working on a project (employed or voluntary) that lasts for months or years. You might be the 'taxi' who ferries children from one extra-curricular activity to another. Your commitment to something, someone or somewhere may even exist after your death, for example through a legacy donation. Commitment can therefore last for moments, for your whole life, in the event of your death and all that lies in between.

What are you currently committed to?

It may be what is on your growing to-do list or in your diary. It could be what has been expressed in a strategy document or an idea that is emerging in your mind. Make a note of the things you have taken on recently or those that are for the future. Include commitments that are personal and professional (you may want to use different coloured pens). Group them into short, medium or long-term commitments so that you can see (and keep track of) what is coming up as well as close to hand.

I have shared my own example with you on page 42. Remember that every commitment has its own timescale, terms of reference and tenure, whichever of the five domains they are in.

Looking through my example I can see that I am doing what is most important to me in terms of my wellbeing, family lifestyle and the work I do. I feel satisfied that my commitments are in proportion across my whole life. If this were not the case, I would consider what to adjust and why. Then I would make small changes over a realistic timescale.

What do your commitments tell you about your leadership in each of the five domains?

Are you satisfied with the proportion of commitments across all areas of your life? Why?

What small changes might you need to make? Over what realistic timescale would you make such changes?

TYPES OF COMMITMENT

As leaders we relate to commitment in our own way. How do I know this? If we were to compare our definition and lists of commitments, we might see similarities but they would not be exactly the same. Despite the differences I have noticed in my work with leaders their commitment usually shows up in four ways:

Read on for stories that demonstrate each one.

NON COMMITMENT

ALANNA'S STORY

I have been contacted by many enthusiastic leaders who are looking for a mentor coach to guide them as they move to and navigate the next level. Alanna was one such leader.

I received her enquiry via email and in the message she described her current situation. Over time I have learned to read between the lines of introductions and what became apparent to me was that she was on the verge of the next level but hesitating for some reason. I suggested dates and times when we could have an initial phone call. With the arrangements made I looked forward to speaking with Alanna.

A day before the call, she postponed it and I began to feel that we had started playing a game of virtual 'hide and seek'. We rearranged for another date and time. On the next occasion we spoke briefly; she said she was 'soooo sorry' and during the conversation it appeared she was ready to go forward. I sent her the relevant documentation, which she returned promptly having signed it.

On the morning of the first session, she emailed to say that something had come up at the last minute so she was unable to attend the session but would be in contact soon. Soon never came and, despite my emailing Alanna several times, I did not hear from her again.

I do not know what stopped Alanna, but I have some idea about the obstacles she may have faced. At the next level obstacles are like mental hurdles we go over, emotional brick walls we demolish or behavioural hoops we jump through. Why? Obstacles are a natural part of giving and making commitment. They are not bad per se, though it may not feel like that when you encounter them. How can obstacles be useful to us?

They slow us down if we are impulsive and make us think more deeply if we are over-busy. They reveal underlying emotions and behaviours that undermine us. They can sabotage our success if we leave them unchecked. The obstacles that arise reveal how we really feel about the commitment we have made or are about to make.

Everyone struggles with different obstacles depending on their life experiences. Some of these may date back to your early life. They remind you that you are a work in progress no matter what level you have reached. Obstacles reveal what is still to learn and what room there is for personal and professional growth. Leaders develop resilience but obstacles can still stop our progress, if we allow them to.

It is critical that you are aware of what sets you back as you seek to make an initial commitment and then keep it for the duration. However, awareness is not enough – we must take action to overcome them too.

How do you feel and behave when faced with commitment?

The twelve common obstacles

I have identified twelve recurring obstacles that may stop you progressing to the next leadership experience. See pages 48 to 49.

You do not have to wait to overcome all the obstacles before you take up the next challenge. It is most likely that you will deal with them as you go along. Identifying the obstacles that are stopping you is the most important thing at this stage. Then you can go on to find and/or create You-shaped solutions to overcome them.

It might seem like a risky strategy but at the next level you will be building on what you have done before. You never start with a 'blank page'. Rest assured that whatever you are going to take on will have been done by another leader even if it is in another domain. Look for such role models in the media, in biographies or make a list of the people who are an inspiration to you in different fields. It may surprise you how many there are.

Assess your obstacles

I relate to all of these obstacles because I have faced them at different times during my leadership journey. They come with the territory and some are easier to overcome than others; it all depends on who you are and how you deal with them. However, you may find that you keep coming up against the same one or more obstacles. Let me give you an example.

While writing this book someone offered me a BIG opportunity in publishing to do something that will take me to the next level in my professional practice, where I am seen as a leader. I was excited by this invitation and scared, but I felt the inner urge strongly so knew that it was an important commitment to consider.

OBSTACLE	WHAT YOU SAY
1. LIFE CIRCUMSTANCES	• I have too much going on right now! I don't have the capacity for any more
2. INNER PERFECTIONIST	• I'll be no good at this. Anyway, I don't have everything in place to do my best
3. WORN OUT	• I am so tired and want to rest. Stop the world – I am getting off for a while
4. FEELING DEMOTIVATED	• I can't be bothered and it requires a lot of effort. What's in it for me?
5. EXISTING RELATIONSHIPS	• I'll lose true and honest friendships that really matter to me. Who else can I trust?
6. FEELING UNSAFE	• Leaving the comfort zone makes me feel insecure. The discomfort will be too much
7. NEGATIVE PERCEPTION	• The next level is going to be so much tougher. Others have failed, so will I
8. MENTAL CONFUSION	• I feel so overwhelmed I don't know what to do first. Perhaps it's not for me
9. PUTTING THINGS OFF	• It can wait, besides I need to figure out exactly what I'll be doing, where and when
10. CHANGE FATIGUE	• I'm fed up with the constant starting and stopping. I'll have to begin all over again
11. ISM'S sexism, ageism, racism, tokenism	• I'd rather not deal with the conflicting, complex and competing systemic issues
12. VISIBILITY	• I don't like being in the limelight and would much rather stay hidden

WHAT I SAY	OVERCOME IT
• Be open minded because this opportunity may be exactly what you need to do next	• Relook at your priorities. What is not as important now as it used to be?
• You're feeling insecure and something is gnawing away at your self-belief. What is it?	• See this as an invitation or experiment rather than a test you have to get right
• You need to recharge your 'batteries' first	• Clarify your work-life balance needs and then stick rigidly to them
• More pressure will wear you down further	• What will motivate you now? The answers to this question will shift inertia
• You are bored, stuck or have lost the 'fire in your belly', which is the drive you'll need	• It is possible to keep your existing relationships and make new ones
• You'll meet lots of amazing people, expand your networks and make new lifelong friends	• Staying in a zone becomes small and will feel like being imprisoned. Let go!
• You have so much untapped potential to release. What safeguards are needed?	• Reframing how you perceive the next level will change your experience
• It won't always be easy but it won't always be as hard as you might expect	• The fog will lift and clarity will come as you start taking small actions
• The assignment is always You-shaped. No one else can do it except for you. Don't panic!	• You are concerned about lots of things. Write a list of the cons and the pros
• Waiting for the 'right' time may result in you missing out on an amazing one-off experience	• Manage your expectations and plan your approach to thrive in this change
• Change is usually incremental rather than seismic, so not everything fluctuates at once	• Prepare yourself for the opposition, confrontation and personal attacks
• Many leaders find exposure difficult, but it is the norm. Learn to cope with the scrutiny and criticism, don't let this stop you!	• Seek professional advice from a PR agent or media expert to understand more. Work with a coach or mentor to overcome any visibility issues/fears

Whenever I am faced with BIG opportunities the obstacles that present themselves are:

LIFE CIRCUMSTANCES *Make lifestyle changes and reprioritise so that I have the capacity to take on this new opportunity. This will involve talking to my husband about the potential changes to our lifestyle and how best to plan for and accommodate these.*

FEELING UNSAFE *Leaving this professional comfort zone could lead me into a state of panic at the thought of what taking up this opportunity means e.g. time away from my family, working longer hours and overseas travel. To minimise the panic, I will put safeguards in place such as strict diary management, delegating tasks to my virtual team and forming new partnerships to manage the growing number of client relationships.*

VISIBILITY *The opportunity will definitely raise my profile and take me into new places within the domains that I currently operate in. I will contact my PR agent for help in managing this so that I am selective about what media or speaking opportunities to accept and have a plan to maintain ongoing marketing activities such as social media updates.*

Which of the obstacles can you relate to most? Why? What other obstacles can you add?

Think of a specific and recent commitment that you made. How many obstacles were present? Did you overcome them? How? If not, why?

Go back to the paragraph you wrote about commitment on page 41. What would you take away or add?

If you have first tried by yourself and feel unable to overcome these obstacles, they may be deeply ingrained mentally, emotionally and physically. If so, you are going to need outside help to identify and practise coping strategies. This outside help can be a coach, a mentor, peer support group, counsellor, supervisor, personal trainer, spiritual director or behavioural therapist. These examples are not an exhaustive list; some leaders have them all and more! Outside help will enable you to overcome the obstacles so you can be and do your best. Be patient with yourself, it may take longer than you realise.

Family and friends are, hopefully, good at listening and cheering you up as you go about working things out. Generally speaking, they are not skilled to help you systematically address these obstacles. They are not objective and so can become impatient; this can strain relationships and could damage them irreparably. Find an experienced professional and keep a clear boundary between your personal and professional life for a time.

Leaders who do not shift to the next level may, on occasion, miss the 'open door' but, I believe and have witnessed that, these new experiences are not gone for ever. You may be down on this occasion but you are not out. *The Leader's Call* will sound again. When you are no longer hesitating or holding back but want to proceed, you will.

OVER COMMITMENT

SANJAY'S STORY

A member of an online networking site sent me an urgent referral on behalf of a friend, Sanjay, asking if I was free for fifteen minutes later that day to speak with him. I was available in the afternoon so said yes. Sanjay was late for the appointment but apologised profusely.

He wanted to explore the possibility of our working together and during the video call he seemed keen. While looking at our diaries to secure a date, I can recall Sanjay speaking out loud as he perused his own diary pages: 'What about? Oh no, not then – I think this would work; no, that is already booked.' He complained, 'I can't find availability for the next six months; I've got too much on.'

Sanjay knew that until he reprioritised, he would not be able to make space for the support that he said he needed. When I asked which diary appointments he considered to be a priority, he said all of them. In his mind they were of equal importance and so to move or cancel one was not possible. 'I'll come back to you when my diary is free.' He did not.

Leaders, who have few obstacles, can be in danger of over committing. There is a never-ending stream of causes, projects or scenarios for leaders to be involved with. The unintended consequence is that, having taken on too much, they regret it but feel pressured into continuing. They become unhappy as stress levels and the expectations of others rise.

I can recall a time where I made a commitment

because I wanted to please the person who asked me. It took months before I realised this, by which time I had decided to back out. Thankfully they were very understanding about my decision but that did not stop me feeling really bad about it. Breaking commitments does not always go this smoothly.

This is not the only time that I have found myself in this position. To undo this pattern I have had to work out my capacity in terms of days, hours and minutes. It is not an exact science but it has helped me to say no, when I might have said yes! We leaders can respond impulsively (new opportunities can be very tempting) instead of slowing down to examine our workload properly before saying 'no', 'not now' or 'yes'.

If you have over committed, it is time to reduce your commitments. This can be hard to do because it means you will need to have 'difficult conversations' with others, who may be surprised, hurt or angry on hearing what you have to say. Face to face is always a better way than a letter, email or text to communicate this kind of message. Be calm, clear and patient, towards those who are hearing your 'announcement' for the first time. Give an agreed notice period on your departure and help find a replacement if possible.

What about you?

If you have made commitments after weighing up the infinite number of pros and cons, that is great. When you can say yes without regrets seconds later, bravo! While this does happen, it is a rarity. Many leaders do not like to say no, or know how to say it without appearing defensive or 'feeble'. If you have a moment of panic or feel like you are screaming 'nooooo' inside, ask for some time to consider what is being asked of you.

If the word yes left your mouth before you could stop it from being heard, ask for a probation period so that you can try it out and see how it goes. You may surprise yourself and be the right leader for the task...others can see our potential, talents and skills even when we cannot. If it does not work out then at least you have tried, others will see that you have tried, and you can move on without regrets or wondering 'What if?'

Putting boundaries in place while leading is critical; there is so much to do and much more you could do. Boundaries are designed to 'ring-fence' your capacity in terms of time, your energy and the resources at your disposal. You simply cannot do everything all the time so choose carefully what is inside and outside your remit. Revisit your boundaries as you move to the next level to make room for what is on the way.

If the problem is open-ended commitments with no deadline or tangible closure, this can leave leaders frustrated. It is because of our concern (and obsession) with adding measurable value wherever we are and whatever we do. If you are facing this, diarise regular reviews of what you are doing. Ask yourself what else you can do here – include others if necessary. If the honest answer is nothing, do not stay on because others want you to or because they like you; have your exit strategy ready. The next level is coming.

Fewer commitments do not mean a leader is less committed. A smaller number can mean you are just as committed – and smarter. Do not compete with other leaders and take on more commitments so that you are seen to have a 'bigger plate'...less can be more!

START STOP COMMITMENT

JOCELYN'S STORY

The first meeting went well. Jocelyn was clear about what she wanted to achieve and by when. She knew The Leader's Call *was taking her to the next level of her leadership experience; she was both apprehensive and excited.*

Before we met, Jocelyn had been prompt in her communication, emailing and texting me with the information she had agreed to share. She completed her 'homework' and was early for the initial conversation. We booked a date and time for session two, in a month's time. Forty-eight hours before the session she cancelled with no explanation, so we rearranged for the following month. That session went ahead and so did the third.

A week before the fourth session, she cancelled again. We rearranged and she cancelled that appointment asking if we could meet two months later. I was frustrated and concerned about the loss of momentum so tried to get to the bottom of what had gone on.

I had no success and after reminding Jocelyn about the agreement conditions (which she had signed) she decided, there and then, to stop the programme without any explanation (even though I asked).

However, Jocelyn did return, a few months later and completed the programme. Why? She decided it was more important to keep on investing in herself and push through the challenges rather than be stopped by them. Jocelyn is flourishing at the next level!

The inner urge will compel you to start taking action of some kind. It could be starting a process of inner enquiry to answer the questions that will not leave your heart or head! You might journal whatever you are feeling and thinking to see what patterns, connections and themes emerge; or you may prefer to learn as you go.

Working through the benefits and pitfalls of a new opportunity in conversations might be your preferred approach. You may have an established inner circle of people whom you trust and who know you. They are your 'go-to group', a sounding board of friends who are not afraid to challenge as well as support you in your time of need.

At the same time, there are downsides to talking solely with people who know you well. Unfortunately, they may have a limited view of your potential, they may not fully understand the context and challenge, or they may (for many reasons) want you to stay where you are. Bringing in an 'outsider' to challenge your perspective might be the best option if you really are serious about moving to the next level and staying there.

ONGOING COMMITMENT

ODETTE'S STORY

Odette was like the majority of leaders I had worked with: focused, energetic and ambitious. She wanted to take a logical and systematic look at the pros and cons of several new opportunities before deciding which to take on.

We were able (unusually for leaders) to book two sessions in her diary with two months between. She wanted to prioritise the sessions and give herself the time to do the research and exploration. Odette had told me this was required to make an informed choice about which domain to lead in and what level of responsibility she wanted to negotiate.

She was a busy leader with multiple and demanding commitments in and outside of work. At times, Odette felt stressed and overwhelmed with all that was going on in and around her. It was not possible for her to be on top of everything in the way she would have liked but she knew this and came to accept that it was simply the way it was. Taking a deep breath in and out, 'All I can do is my best' was her constant refrain.

Due to her increasing workload and lack of support there were a few times when Odette wanted to pull out of the programme. However, on reviewing her progress, she noticed the learning and tangible achievements she had gained which spurred her on. She completed the programme and followed up two opportunities: one that she had prior experience of and the other she was curious about.

THE REALITIES OF LEADERSHIP

None of the above leaders' stories are right or wrong, to be desired or to be avoided. They simply illustrate how real leaders, from the newbies to more experienced, relate to commitment and react when faced with it. I do not know if the way these four leaders behaved when working with me was an example of how they behave in their daily personal or professional lives. It is possible, but only they or others who see them behave in private and public over time can be the judge of that.

I am aware that we do not always know how committed we are or can be until we make the commitment. What can you do?

Multiple conversations with different stakeholders or shadowing and probation periods can help to an extent. Whether you have a business or are leading in the community or around the world, you have to do your research thoroughly. Find out as much as you can before you make a choice. The leaders' stories I have shared remind us that you need to be responsive, motivated and determined when making and keeping a commitment.

You will require these attributes in small or large doses to see you through to the end of the next level and on to the levels beyond. I hope that the leaders' stories here enable you to consider what your tendency is when it comes to your commitment-making approach, whether in personal or professional situations, or both.

So far, we have defined commitment, reviewed the different responses by leaders to it, and identified common obstacles and how to overcome them. Revisit your definition of commitment, on page 41, and see if you feel you would like to make any amendments. Then complete the following exercise to create a mini mission statement – it can be a sentence or paragraph. I have included my own as an example.

GRACE'S STATEMENT OF COMMITMENT...

When I am committed to moving to the next level it means, I am ready and willing to do whatever it takes to up my leadership game so that I can make the world a better place

STATEMENT OF COMMITMENT

When I am committed to moving to the next level it means, I...

....
....
....
....
....
....
....
....
....
....
....
....

MANIFEST YOUR COMMITMENT

As you make your way to the next level it can take a
while to figure out what your commitment 'looks like'. To
give you some idea, read on for what happened to me.

On reaching Heathrow Airport following my trip
to Ghana, I scanned a copy of *New African* magazine
in a newsagent shop. Once again I was excited
and impressed at the stories of positive change in
infrastructure, economy, people power, leadership and
entrepreneurial spirit across Africa. On this occasion
the inner urge felt almost primal. It was the singer
Angelique Kidjo who said that an African is always
confronted by the question of how they can give back to
the continent. I was being confronted.

To discover answers to the questions of how I could
make a contribution to Ghana and the continent of Africa
and what did I have to offer, I entered a period of deep
contemplation and introspection. This did not mean
that I moved to a distant island and became a hermit!
I continued to live and work, but it was as if a part of
me was shut off to the world and in retreat. I started to
write about this whole experience in my journal.

Around this time, I began to review my business and
realised that I had achieved the vision and exceeded the
goals I had created for myself between 2003 and 2013.
I felt it was time to go back to the basics in my life and
work. I began to form a new personal and professional
vision: a compelling and vivid mental image of what
I was hoping to achieve over the next decade. Such a
vision is a destination point encapsulating your targets,
goals and intentions. It will energise and excite you as

you move to the next level of your leadership experience.

I call any vision that I create in words or images 'Plan B'! Why? Firstly, no one can predict the future in its minutiae. Secondly, vision needs to be flexible so that you can update it as you move to the next level. Any vision needs to be revisited and adapted to the constant change that occurs in and around the five domains of leadership.

In addition to the journaling and vision activities, I started a conversation with my husband and we talked about taking a family gap year in Africa. I contacted Voluntary Service Overseas (VSO) about volunteering and applied for two jobs in international development, which seemed to me to be the sector that most closely aligned with the contribution I wanted to offer to make a difference and give something back.

Although I had been trustee of a small NGO in Ghana, it was still in its start-up phase so my contacts in the international development sector were few. In the past, when I have wanted to create relationships in new sectors and industries, I have turned to my network. However, at this stage it drew a blank, there was no one I could talk to or who could guide my efforts.

At some point during this flurry of activity I remembered a conversation I had had with a financial director, whose next level had involved transitioning from the private sector to the charity sector. He had attended a charity information event. So I looked up the organisers and registered to attend a one-hour introduction to the charity sector.

During that hour I felt the inner urge intensely, as if it was saying to me 'yes, this is your next level!'. I was excited and full of joy! This organisation had a list of mentors with extensive knowledge and experience of the charity and international development sector. I asked to see a few mentor profiles and selected one because it 'ticked all the boxes' of what I was looking for. The thing that stood out most of all was that my potential mentor was a life-long learner which is one of my core leadership values.

In time, I was introduced to Jacqueline Hill and after one meeting we agreed to work together: me as the mentee, her as the mentor. Jacqueline was fantastic in helping me to understand where the inner urge was taking me (she had experienced it numerous times herself). I was encouraged to do whatever I felt was necessary to answer the questions I had. As I experimented, the mental fog lifted.

Over the coming weeks and months I sensed that the contribution I could make to Africa was not in a family gap year or a full-time role for an international development organisation. It was being intentional on equipping leaders in the sector to increase their impact further so that the world could become a better place more quickly.

After all the effort I had made this conclusion was not frustrating or disappointing. It had always been about exploring possibilities and eliminating those that were not the right fit for me, rather than going for instant gratification. It can take time, patience and courage to turn your commitment into action, but you get there in the end.

GOOD THINGS COME TO THOSE WHO COMMIT

When you take the leap and move to the next level (whether you know precisely what that is or not), something magical and powerful starts to happen. In stepping out, I started to receive what I call 'blessings', which came in the form of people, invitations and resources. Some people see this as the law of attraction, synchronicity or serendipity.

Here are some of the amazing blessings I received:

- My mentor introduced me to one of her contacts at a global international development organisation that does work all over the world including Africa. Our initial conversation revealed many shared interests in the area of leadership development. This organisation is now one of my clients and the services that I designed and delivered for them (based on my leadership development expertise) has turned into a product that I am taking to other organisations that are making the world a better place.

- A peer and new friend introduced me to the then deputy chair of an Africa-based international development organisation that was looking for new trustees. This in turn led to me being interviewed jointly by the founder and CEO. They invited me to join the board as a non-executive director. This organisation is leading the field in the education of rural girls and women in Zimbabwe, Zambia, Ghana, Tanzania and Malawi!

- While attending a conference I met a kindred spirit and we shared our leadership stories. On the back of our meeting, she asked if she could nominate me to become a fellow of the Royal Society for the encouragement of Arts, Manufactures and Commerce (RSA). After researching the organisation, I said 'yes please!'. Little did I know that months later the RSA would launch a Diaspora ChangeMakers project for African Diaspora Leaders in the UK funded by Comic Relief and Unbound Philanthropy. Sadly my kindred spirit died, but her inspiration lives on.

- The RSA project instantly gave me a Pan-African leadership network. My experiences led me to start up African Diaspora Kids, a community legacy project that is seeking to nurture the social, cultural and leadership potential of primary-school aged children in London. It is a lifelong commitment because the project will run for the next twenty-five years.

- I was also selected as one of a hundred African Diaspora leaders to benefit from a leadership programme designed and delivered by Common Purpose, a global leadership development organisation. One of the staff did some voluntary work for me. In addition to the programme, there were networking events to attend and new relationships to build.

- It so happened, one of the leaders I met on the Common Purpose leadership programme shared my passion for developing African leaders on the continent. We became friends and through her social enterprise, we are piloting a Leadership for Africa programme that so far has been run in Tunisia, Eritrea and Johannesburg, South Africa. The feedback has been very positive and we are exploring ways to make the programme available to more leaders.

When I look back on what has resulted (so far) from my making and keeping commitment at this next level, I am amazed. Confirmation that you are heading in the right direction and doing the right things will encourage you to keep going. There are many blessings waiting for you too!

ACTIONS TO TAKE

The Leader's Call may be taking you into something you have wanted to do for ages but various circumstances have held you back until now. It might be that you have an inkling of what the next level means for you and are ready to figure out the details. Or you might be clueless but resonate strongly with the idea of doing the next thing, whatever it is. All of these are fine.

Discerning your next level is a matter for the heart (what you feel), head (what you think) and hand (what you do). It is a time to experiment and try new things. Then you will know what might work and what might not. Throughout you will be guided by your values – the things that are most important to you – and your intuition. Keep being proactive and remember that everything you do is an act of your commitment.

Schedule time in your diary to do whatever actions are necessary. Begin by choosing at least two things that appeal to you from each list below.

Inner reflection

- Spend regular time in contemplation
- Read about an area of interest and make a note of your insights
- Journal to see what patterns, themes and connections emerge
- Hire a mentor to help you rigorously explore a range of 'what if?' scenarios
- Consider different ideas and see which ones feel right
- Talk to members of your go-to group and record what resonates

Outer reflection

- Contact organisations in the sector/industry you have identified
- Look for role models and learn from them
- Network, network, network!
- Follow up with relevant people from the past
- Go to events in your area of interest
- Apply for jobs and attend interviews

Doing all this is a lot like being a detective, investigating this inner urge and trying to obtain evidence. Follow the trail of your feelings and make notes of the information you gather. It may not seem like it but be encouraged, one step forward and three steps back is making progress!

What I have found is that the wisdom you seek is all around you. You will notice the messages on bags, t-shirts, signposts, windows, billboards and adverts. You will overhear particular words in conversations, see symbols and metaphors, pick up books, read articles and even come across the thing that you need to know while 'distracted' on the internet.

Where there is a will there is a way. Once you start taking action, the world around will offer signs, encouragement and connections to new people, all of which will help guide you towards the next level. It can still take effort, time and energy to 'make the unknown known', but in time the clarity and conviction you have been looking for will turn up, both inside and outside of you.

MOVING ON

I understand that you may be hesitant or resistant to making a commitment without having all the facts. After all, you probably do not know where *The Leader's Call* is going to take you. Whether you trust or not, accept the discomfort or not, can cope with the lack of control or not, get started. Intention or intrigue is enough for things to unfold.

In this chapter, we have examined commitment. I have shared other leaders' stories, explored the obstacles to commitment and ways to overcome them.

I hope that through my experiences and those of other leaders you feel more empowered to stay at the next level and complete what you are there to do.

If you are willing to follow where *The Leader's Call* takes you and progress, let's go forward to insight number two, where A is for Authenticity.

'The first step towards getting somewhere is to decide that you are not going to stay where you are'

Unknown

INSIGHT

2

A

is for

AUTHENTICITY

'Be honest with yourself'

Nelson Mandela

BECOMING WHO YOU ARE

Responding to *The Leader's Call* means it is time to take a truthful look at yourself and come to terms with who you are, who you are not and who you aspire to be at this point of your leadership adventure. Such self-scrutiny and clear feedback from others will enable you to present yourself authentically at the next level for as long as you are there.

In the twenty-first century it is accepted that to be an effective leader you will work towards self-awareness, being real and comfortable in your skin. I call this 'You-shaped leadership'.

Hiding behind a job title, mimicking other leaders, putting on an act or faking it until you make it is not authentic leadership. Authenticity comes when you are willing to discover and rediscover yourself, owning what you discover and leading from your place of uniqueness.

There is much more to you than meets the eye and which goes beyond the first impression. Over time I have come to the conclusion that who you are is a complex blend of the following diverse features (in no particular order).

INNER YOU

1. **Personal:** character, talents, defining moments, abilities, interests, shadow, roles

2. **Emotional:** how you see and feel about yourself and others, and situations

3. **Spiritual:** values that you are deeply passionate about and which strongly motivate and direct you

4. **Relational:** interaction with people in your personal and professional network

5. **Historical:** past and current experiences – the highs, lows and day to day

6. **Generational:** behavioural traits you inherit at home and from other adults

7. **Cultural:** individual, communal, local and global beliefs, rituals and customs

OUTER YOU

1. **Physical:** gender, movement, appearance, voice, presence, the energetic aura you emit

2. **Intellectual:** educational attainment via informal/formal study, alone and with others

3. **Social:** the environments you grew up in and the world events that defined them

4. **Professional:** transferable skills, achievements, failings, strengths, roles, actions

5. **Behavioural:** transfer/application of knowledge, expertise, turning visions into reality

6. **Financial:** resources and opportunities that were or were not available

7. **Vocational:** identifying and doing what only you are on this planet to fulfil

Which of the inner and outer features resonate with you most? Why?

I deliberately split the inner and outer features to reinforce what an original creation you are. Day to day these features intermingle to make you a unique individual and dynamic human being. You are the same, yet different. Parts of you are fixed, others are fluid. We perceive you but we cannot perceive all of you. As you grow through the different stages of human development 'who you are' is visibly and invisibly shifting and being shaped.

The world needs what you have to offer. You are a one-off in the seven billion plus human community on planet Earth. You may have a *doppelgänger* (someone who looks just like you). Others may identify strongly with you because of your life experiences, but no one perceives the world or interacts with it as you do. No one else does exactly what you do in exactly the way you do it. And no one ever will!

In this chapter we will consider what it is to do the work of becoming who you are. It is a process and the leaders' stories will highlight practical ways to go through it. You will come across key questions to which there are no right answers! They are designed to capture your honest feelings and thoughts, so go with your intuition and be spontaneous.

I will share my self-discovery and self-disclosure experiences too. I will suggest actions that will deepen your self-awareness so that you can apply what you have learned from this second insight. All are designed to encourage you to move to the next level when you hear *The Leader's Call*, and to be yourself whatever that means to you.

YOU-SHAPED LEADERSHIP

To be a leader shaped like yourself and not like other leaders you need to be familiar and practised in the process of becoming who you are. There are four stages:

KNOWING	BEING TRUE TO	EXPRESSING	ACCEPTING

YOURSELF

Doing the work that is required at each stage will reveal the core and fringes of your authentic self. It might feel hard at first but your patience will pay off. In time, you will feel more confident, congruent and in tune with yourself. This is vital as you move to a new level within the domains, where you will have multiple roles to play and competing responsibilities to fulfil. Those around you will measure how authentic you are by how consistent you are.

KNOWING YOURSELF

INGRID'S STORY

We had made contact via a third party who told me that Ingrid was going through what seemed to be an identity crisis. She was leaving her current leadership role through no desire of her own: she had been made redundant after decades of faithful service.

When we met for the first time Ingrid looked

vulnerable and near to tears. She had known the
redundancy was coming because, like her peers, she
had to decide on difficult cost reductions in her area
and restructure functions for a third time. As the highly
respected leader of a large business unit, it was the 'we
are letting you go' conversation that made her realise
she had been in denial for months.

Our meeting was the space she longed for to reflect
on decades of being associated with a senior leadership
role and title that had given her a good reputation,
power and influence. When I asked Ingrid to describe
herself, she looked perplexed before going on to say, 'I
don't know who I am anymore. Work dominated my life
and without me noticing, decades have come and gone.'
The way she saw herself was shaped predominately by
the outer self; she had given little thought to who she
was on the inside.

Ingrid's story is not unusual. I have met and worked
with leaders who have never got to know themselves
beyond talking about their personal lives just enough to
give the appearance that they are not overly dedicated
(or attached) to their work persona, even when they are.
Why? For some it is a lack of time to go 'soul-searching'.
Others are more comfortable with their outer self. Many
leaders do not have the 'know-how' to do the work and
for the goal-focused leader it was never required as a
specific goal, so they did not bother.

Leadership has the potential to keep us too busy. We
expend huge amounts of energy and effort delivering
results through strategy implementation, team
performance and resource management, to name a few

of the weekly activities that leaders are expected to do. We can be so focused on our outer self that we neglect the inner self until a crisis, usually not of our making, forces us to stop and get to know ourselves before we proceed further.

What's your backstory?

I asked Ingrid to write a story about her past, going back as far as she liked, focusing on her inner features (see page 71) and describing as many or as few of them as she liked.

The story, I told her, could be long or short. Because it was for her own use, I advised her to write freely (by hand or using a computer) not worrying about grammatical mistakes or factual errors. Perfectionism was not required for this activity! This first draft of her story was designed to be a 'brain dump', so that she could 'see herself' on paper to understand her own story to date and acknowledge it. The good, bad and challenging!

The inner features that resonated most with Ingrid were:

2. **Emotional:** how you see and feel about yourself and others, and situations

5. **Historical:** past and current experiences – the highs, lows and day to day

When I asked why this was, she replied, 'I think these are core parts of my identity. Writing about them will help me reconnect with who I am in a new way.' Ingrid had become disconnected from her emotional self and did not pay much attention to how she felt. She added that putting her story into chronological order would clarify her distant and recent past.

We had to go back to basics so that Ingrid could develop a stronger inner self for the future, whatever it held. She came to believe that in a strange way the redundancy was a positive thing and a blessing in disguise. Ingrid was committed to putting her leadership abilities to use. She decided not to retreat but instead go forward into the unknown.

Ingrid had been forced out of her comfort zone and otherwise would not have willingly moved to the next level. Wisely, instead of talking to those who had already contacted her with a range of leadership opportunities, Ingrid decided to take quality time out so that she would not be interrupted or distracted from the necessary task – that of knowing herself.

Ingrid took one month to complete the story activity. During that time, she sent me several emails commenting on how difficult it was 'being with herself'. In the first week she procrastinated and used her time to prioritise other things from meeting up with ex-colleagues, having long lunches, visiting family to completing domestic chores.

Her breakthrough came after she sat down in front of a blank page one afternoon. Rather fortuitously I had felt moved to send her an email that very morning which said 'keep going, don't give up!'. On this occasion, rather than run away from the empty page Ingrid wrote what came to her using some of the inner you features as a starting point.

A week later she emailed me again to say how amazed she was at discovering who she was! For years Ingrid lacked self-belief because she underestimated her achievements – a list much longer than she imagined.

There was a mismatch between how she saw herself and who she really was. She had received very little positive and constructive feedback from her line manager or peers, so she had not noticed the enormous difference she made.

Ingrid had felt it nigh on impossible not to write about her outer self, which had defined her for so many years. (As I have said the inner and outer selves are an integral part of each other.) However, she courageously kept a focus on the parts of herself she was less familiar with. Writing as much as possible, she used words like 'sensitive', 'kind', 'supportive'. She was 'trusted', 'an advisor', 'pioneering', 'a leader', 'trouble shooter' and 'entrepreneurial'. These were all new ways of describing herself and a true reflection.

Having written her story down, she looked amongst the text for specific examples to support these words. Although such examples are based on your own perspective, feeding back to yourself is a good place to start.

While reading Ingrid's written piece I became teary eyed at the thought that this was a part of her which had been unintentionally covered up, hidden away and even dominated by the outer self. She sounded happy and hopeful. It struck me how easy it is to go through life not knowing who we are.

We met again when the month was up and talked about how she was doing. The comment that has stuck with me is when Ingrid said, 'Now that I have gotten to know myself, I don't want to ever forget.' To prevent history repeating itself she came up with the idea of writing a personal and professional story at the end of each year to capture the shifting and shaping that was taking place within and outside her.

Months after we had stopped working together Ingrid

emailed me to say she had indeed moved to the next level of her leadership experience. She was accepting a leadership role with a larger team, greater resources and lots of international travel. She felt able to take the job because she had confidence in who she was and what she could do. I congratulated her, signing off with 'remember to keep on getting to know yourself!'.

Which of the inner features would you write a story about? Why? Write your own story – either in longhand or on a computer; write as much or as little as you wish.

BEING TRUE TO YOURSELF

There will be many times in leadership when you are faced with a struggle between what you value and believe and what others want you to value and believe. I have observed that authentic leaders are those who genuinely try to be who they are and at the same time try to do what is best for others. Leadership is doing what others need you to do so they can realise and express their leadership abilities not just so you can exercise leadership.

RYAN'S STORY

Being relatively new to leadership, Ryan was experiencing his first inner battle. He had wanted the promotion that took him to this foundation level of his leadership experience. He had had it in his sights ever since starting out as a volunteer at the social enterprise. Achieving the promotion was a reward for his efforts. The inner battle was not about the work he had to do as his technical specialism was what he enjoyed, even

*loved. His struggle was with how to be true to himself
while working alongside his new team, line manager,
peers and all the other stakeholders with whom he
had new relationships.*

*Ryan was a highly self-aware leader who
enjoyed reading self-help books and completing
self-assessment questionnaires so he could know
what made him 'tick'. This awareness led him out of
one organisation where he had felt constrained into
another where he felt liberated. He regularly asked
those he trusted in his personal and professional
network for specific feedback so as to stay connected
with what was most important to him at home and in
the workplace. Ryan had 'done the work' to nurture a
strong inner self.*

*After searching online, he had come across my
website and sent me a message about the possibility
of our working together. During our conversation he
demonstrated that, while he recognised the inner
battle, he did not know what practically to do about
it. He was fearful that this feeling might lead him to
resign from this organisation. When he mentioned the
term 'conflict of values', I knew he had recognised the
crux of his dilemma.*

With Ryan having already done a lot of hard work
getting to know himself this was not his main concern
when we agreed to start working together. He was clear
about who he was and who he was not: 'pretending was
not an option' he told me. His intention was to manage
the balance between being true to himself with being
true to the organisation.

As we talked, it became clear that the struggle was not about what was expected of him by the organisation in terms of achieving targets or upping his performance. It was not about relating to his peers; being outgoing and friendly, he found it easy to get along with most, even difficult, people. His struggle was with the culture of the organisation and how things were being done to get results.

The conflict of values he felt was in the spiritual part of his inner self. Ryan was proud of his moral compass and had rarely given in to the many temptations to be, say or do anything he would regret. He knew about leaders who 'had their price', whether money or power, that would sway them to say or do what was expected of them by others. Such leaders become inauthentic.

Overheard comments made by a senior leader at the end of a confrontational interdepartmental meeting had alarmed Ryan, especially because he respected and sought to emulate this senior leader. The comments had given Ryan an impression (he admitted that it might be an assumption) that in order for him to stay at his level or progress he might have to compromise his values and become someone he did not want to be.

Ryan and I created a range of different scenarios that he felt would overtly and subtly put his spiritual values and ethics to the test. He then worked through all the potential responses he could make by writing them out and through role play with a trained actor, who brilliantly played the characters of different stakeholders in Ryan's sphere of influence.

Interestingly, it was during the role playing that Ryan had a breakthrough moment. He understood that he could pick his battles and compromise on some things without 'losing himself' spiritually, ethically or morally. There was space for him to stand his ground without appearing narrow-minded, self-righteous and intractable. He did not have to conform to and collude with the cultural status quo, instead he could challenge it. Ryan was relieved!

At the end of our time working together Ryan had exhausted all the possible situations and circumstances that he had felt uncomfortable with. While he knew that something unexpected might happen, he was confident in having developed a way of discerning how to 'stick' or 'adapt'. He could still be true to himself, fulfil his role and be successful.

Leading with authenticity

Authenticity is like a hallmark, watermark or a trademark. It is particular to you and cannot be copied or replicated. Your authenticity is not only revealed through your behaviour, personality and values, but also through your quirks and idiosyncrasies. Your authentic self is always present whether you are in a public arena or private space.

Leaders doing what they like and how they like without considering the consequences will be led down the path of irresponsibility. With leadership comes power and control. Someone once told me that leaders are always being watched; I think this is true. Who is watching you?

You have the ability to significantly influence others, positively and negatively, directly and indirectly through what you say and do or don't say and do? Who we are being or not being can unwittingly give others permission to do the same. In the introduction to this book I made the point that we can no longer tell those around us what to do and then be something else. This is a lack of integrity and breeds double standards, which 'followers' in particular will rail against, in private and in public.

While the ending of Ryan's story is a happy one, it may not be the case for other leaders. It takes maturity to work through situations like this and stay with the discomfort rather than take what seems to be an easy option and walk or run away. What you need to know is that situations like this will come again and again in the complex realm of the five domains. It is therefore better for you to learn sooner rather than later how to deal with them directly.

Sadly, because they do not have the 'know-how' there are leaders who relinquish their moral compass and others who lower their ethical standards seeming to give permission for a whole range of undesirable behaviours to flourish and situations to go unchallenged. Some leaders may choose to stick their heads in the sand hoping that dilemmas will go away. They will not.

The benefit of working with outside helpers, which on this occasion involved a mentor, coach and actor, meant that Ryan was challenged to widen his perspective, explore multiple outcomes (including difficult ones) and understand the potential and unintended consequences of what he might do or not do. This ability would stand him in good stead to be true to himself at whatever level of leadership experience he moved to in future.

When did you face a situation that forced you to consider if you were being true to yourself? What did you do?

EXPRESSING YOURSELF

YOLANDA'S STORY

Yolanda and I had met years previously following the publication of my first book The Career Itch – 4 Steps for Taking Control of What You Do Next. *Yolanda was what you might call a 'high flyer'. She had progressed quickly, going to the top of the career ladder and beyond it. Now she was preparing herself for what was coming next, and when I talked about* The Leader's Call *she shrieked, saying it described exactly what she was going through.*

Her commitment to going wherever The Leader's Call *was taking her was clear. She had started out as a reluctant leader and sought outside help to work through the anxiety she had had about leading others. Over many years she had gone from being a fearful leader to an outstanding one. Now she was very excited about what the future held.*

Yolanda's experience of moving from one leadership level to the next had provided ample chances for her to know herself more deeply and be true to herself. She had worked alongside many leaders with different styles and had come through a wide range of testing situations and high pressure circumstances. She had raised her self-esteem and self-confidence by stepping out of what she was familiar with into what was unfamiliar.

As we talked, Yolanda explained that the numerous issues thrown up by working across the five domains of leadership had honed her authentic self, not harmed it. She was no longer afraid of the challenging environment. Instead of trying to escape it, she allowed it to test who she was being and what she was doing. Yolanda was able to harness the conditions so that they worked in her favour. She had become comfortable in her skin.

Having been an employee, then a freelancer, while taking on caring responsibilities for a period of time, she was ready to explore what might take her to the next level. She had the feeling that she had come a long way but there was a part of her that had not arrived yet. Something was emerging but it was not yet fully formed.

Letting yourself be seen

Yolanda had aspirations to become more of herself than ever before. This emergent self is like pulling the sheet off a mirror bit by bit: each pull reveals a part of yourself that you may not have seen before. For Yolanda doing the work was not about looking back or looking into her current situation, it was about looking forward into what might be.

When we talked about all the ideas that were 'popping up' in her heart and mind it became clear that Yolanda's aspirations were many and multiplying! She decided that capturing these ideas together in one place would be helpful before choosing what to hold on to, what to let go of and what to take up at the next level.

Moving through a number of transitions has taught me that you cannot rush your emergent self into being; it takes its own time. I can be very impatient, so developing the ability to wait and see can feel excruciating. Sharing my own transition frustrations allowed Yolanda to realise that she had also experienced trying to rush the process to reach a destination. On this occasion, she opted to go slowly and keep the pace.

In the meantime, she looked for and found an interim role that, while demanding, was not as stressful and highly pressured as her other leadership roles. This gave her space and time to capture ideas as they came. Nine months later she presented me with what she referred to as her 'leadership portrait'. It was an A3 sheet covered with a creative collage of photographs, textures, shapes, metaphors, quotes, words, colours, symbols and numbers.

As Yolanda pointed to various parts of the portrait she accepted that she could not logically or rationally explain everything in it. She was okay with that. Instead of judging what she had produced, Yolanda decided to be content with her lack of insight and understanding. She had expressed herself and that was enough at this embryonic stage. Making sense and taking action, she believed and trusted, would come later.

It was this 'simple' and childlike creative activity that showed a part of Yolanda that she had not been able to see for herself or talk about with others.

What new self is trying to emerge inwardly and outwardly for you? How can you express it creatively? Try, for example, a collage, mood board, random words, a poem, story etc.

ACCEPTING YOURSELF

KIM LEE'S STORY

We introduced ourselves and got talking during one of the breaks at an event. A mentor to new leaders, Kim Lee told me she defined authenticity as her ability to be self-critical, in a positive and empowering way. When I shared with her the list of inner and outer features I had identified over time, Kim Lee told me that she did not resist looking more deeply at her inner and outer self as her desire was to be as self-aware as possible. Her commitment to this meant she was working with a coach and mentor.

Kim Lee had become a leader when strengths-based leadership was the 'in thing'. This approach meant that she tended to focus on what was positive about herself and the leadership experience, while ignoring what was less positive. This ability to 'celebrate' was welcomed by some of her mentees but others found that only looking at strengths was superficial.

Conversations with others helped Kim Lee to admit that she had been working at a surface level because that is where she was most comfortable. She was scared of working 'at depth' for fear of being unable to support her mentees properly and answer their difficult questions. Kim Lee had been avoiding the most challenging and potentially most meaningful and rewarding experiences of her mentees and of her own leadership.

Your true nature

As you move to the next level of your leadership experience, you may not always be aware of the impact that the unstable nature of the five domains of leadership has on you. What you think, do and say at one level is not always what you will think, do and say at the next. The domains give rise to conditions that 'pull and push' your character to reveal aspects of the inner you that up until that point had been latent. Leaders have told me how in some circumstances they were surprised and shocked at their behaviour.

Leaders are like every other human being. You have the capacity to go from being selfless to selfish, and all that lies between, in a flash. This shows up moment by moment through countless, everyday interactions in the public space at work and in the private space at home. To be an effective leader does not require you to know all the ins and outs of what it means to be fully human.

However, you need some expertise in the breadth and depth of what it means to be human. Why? When all is said and done, the heart of leadership is about human relationships and making things happen through them. Pause for a moment and think about it. Leadership is about people: women, men and children. It is about how and why you relate to yourself in the way you do. It is about how and why you relate to others in the way you do.

Kim Lee's admission gave way to a new curiosity about who she had been, who she was being and who she was becoming. Doing the work, for her, centred on what she enjoyed, which was reading. Kim Lee read articles on a range of topics including anthropology, history, philosophy, sociology, psychology (especially Transactional Analysis) and neuroscience. She said, 'Becoming the best leader and mentor I can be means it is time to embrace my strengths and weaknesses, successes and failings because they are valuable parts of me.'

It takes a courageous leader to willingly look at their imperfections and their 'dark side'. Many of us want to stay at the surface level of ourselves where we feel sure rather than plunge into the unknown depths of our 'humanness'. It is as if we have a default mode that warns us to stay with what we know. However, this mode will not equip us to deal with the inevitably testing situations we will face in our homes and in the world. We can learn important lessons from looking honestly at what goes on inside and outside us every day.

The next time I spoke to Kim Lee, she had some interesting things to tell me: 'All the reading prompted me to write descriptions about different aspects of myself such as what I am good at, what I don't do well, my contradictions and shortcomings. I wrote a list of the types of people I get along with and those who for some reason "press my buttons". I was shocked to work out that I undermine myself and that I can be controlling. I'm still working on accepting that all these descriptions are me. They're what makes me human!'

You will experience the best and worst of times at the next level. Some of that is down to life circumstances running parallel to and colliding with your leadership experiences. Some is down to the nature of change brought about by factors way beyond your control. When you are able to accept yourself and be more transparent with others authenticity is possible, whether you are leading through triumphs or tribulations. Treating yourself gently, with forgiveness and compassion will enable you to treat others the same way.

What features of your inner and outer self do you find it easy and/or difficult to accept? Why?

SHOWING UP FROM THE INSIDE OUT

When I worked as an employee in the 1980s and 90s I did not think about being authentic. Back then it was not talked about or seen as being desirable. I tried to emulate those in my peer group who were identified and held up as being, saying and doing the right thing in the right way. I was trying to fit into another person's skin (not a nice image!). I was trying to be shaped like others not shaped like me.

Thankfully, change in many organisations now means the emphasis is on authenticity not uniformity. Organisations want cultures that are heterogeneous not homogenous. In my last employed role, the organisation was very diverse in terms of culture, background and ability – it was one of the reasons why I wanted to work there. I felt more like myself in that role: not only because of the people around me but because I was growing in self-awareness, self-expression and self-acceptance.

Starting a business meant that I no longer had a brand to 'hide' behind, so I created my own: Grace Owen Solutions Ltd. I can remember struggling with what to call the business. I had lots of ideas but none of them felt right. It was only when I used my own name that something clicked. I did not see it at the time but now I know that the saying 'people buy people' is true. My clients work with me because of who I am.

Like a butterfly going through different stages of metamorphosis it has taken me time to be at ease (though still not a hundred per cent comfortable!) with self-disclosure. I have undergone at least five brand reinventions – each one has refined my authenticity. I think self-discovery is the easy bit! If you are a business owner and struggling with visibility, do not attempt to go all out at once. Try different marketing mixes and find what works best for you. I have settled on online networking sites, one-to-one networking and PR. I am yet to move into the world of communicating within 140 characters!

During 2012 to 2015, as I moved from and to the next level, I unknowingly engaged in multiple ways of taking a truthful look at myself. I probed more deeply at who I had been, was being and becoming. I got to know myself and started being true to myself. I found media for expressing myself. I learned to accept the parts of me that I felt saddened and ashamed about instead of wishing I was not like that. This is still a challenge for me.

All of this has amounted to making me a more honest, real and transparent leader. I am no longer overly worried about whether others like me or not. I am no longer trying to be someone that I am not. I no longer try to fit into others' skins. I am who I am and I love myself! This has given me the ability to be more compassionate and more effective in my work. The leaders I meet are also struggling to become who they are and to be authentic.

All of the inner and outer features on pages 71 to 72 are parts of my authenticity and what I noticed is that all of these came to the surface following my experience on that road in Accra, Ghana. Why? I think it is because I needed to do a complete review of myself so that I could become more of who I am. You can see below how I did this for each of the inner and outer features.

INNER ME

1. **Personal: character, talents, defining moments, abilities, interests, shadow, roles**

   I completed numerous leadership and career self-assessments. I also asked for feedback from twenty-five people from all the domains of leadership who knew me well and whom I knew would be honest and compassionate. Each assessment provided a report that I read and analysed to identify overarching themes about the shifts in this part of me.

2. **Emotional: how you see and feel about yourself and others, and situations**

   Having kept a journal for years (written by hand and on my laptop) I was able to document the weird, wonderful, unsettling and uplifting life experiences that I was going through. Experiencing the death of both my parents, which led to rifts in the family domain, led me to meet with a bereavement counsellor to explore the issues and my grief.

3. **Spiritual: values that you are deeply passionate about and which strongly motivate and direct you**

   I have four values – connection, care, community and contribution – that anchor how I live and lead my life. I revisited what these meant to me and considered how they might look over the next decade. To consolidate my ideas, I wrote a life vision with the goals I am working towards. I call it 'Plan B' because I cannot predict what will or won't happen.

4. **Relational: interaction with people in your personal and professional network**

The diverse network of people that has grown around me is captured in the mobile devices I use, an address book (not electronic) and on social media platforms. What I noticed is how some of these relationships came to the fore and others moved into the background. I began to forge new relationships and collaborations.

5. **Historical: past and current experiences – the highs, lows and day to day**

Working with a new client allowed me to look back on the significant experiences of my life, career and leadership experiences. I learned that all the experiences have made me who and what I am.

There were moments of joyous celebration and times of deepening my self-awareness and growth, personally and professionally.

6. **Generational:** behavioural traits you inherit at home and from other adults

I too have said, 'I'm becoming like my father!' or 'I'm becoming like my mother!'. It is not surprising that at various times we behave like the adults who were around during the formative moments of our life, whether at birth, puberty, adolescence or when we made big strides in our adult life. However, there are traits I would like to leave with them!

7. **Cultural:** individual, communal, local and global beliefs, rituals and customs

Travelling to West, North, South and East Africa during my leadership transition exposed my cultural DNA. I experienced things first hand and heard second hand from Pan African leaders about cultural similarities and differences across the continent.

OUTER ME

1. **Physical:** gender, movement, appearance, voice, presence, the energetic aura you emit

Alongside doing the inner work, I revisited an old report by an image consultant to assess how my 'look' was changing to better reflect the inner and outer me. I hired a new consultant to redesign the business brand. In time, I launched a new website and printed new business cards, which I gave away when networking and socialising!

2. **Intellectual: educational attainment via informal/ formal study, alone and with others**

   While I did not feel it necessary to retrain during this transition, there were many opportunities for me to learn informally. I read lots of different types of material, visited arts and culture spaces and events. I networked with people I did not know so well and found every conversation was a learning experience. I developed at my own pace.

3. **Social: the environments you grew up in and the world events that defined them**

   My sister Rose and I visited places where we had lived and gone to school. We recalled happy memories and winced with embarrassment at difficult ones. We noted how our world as teenagers (no internet or social media) and adults (introduction of email and computers in the workplace) had radically changed us.

4. **Professional: transferable skills, achievements, failings, strengths, roles, actions**

   I have been fortunate to belong to a continuing

professional development (CPD) group for over
five years. We are six business owners who
work independently and collaboratively across
every sector and in every industry developing
individuals, teams, groups and organisations. We
have a fabulous supervisor who 'holds' a safe
space in which we grow.

5. **Behavioural:** transfer/application of knowledge,
    expertise, turning visions into reality
    Early on in my leadership experience I was
    'over-busy'. As a result, I was productive and
    labelled as a high performer. Despite being able
    to see and keep in mind the bigger picture I did
    not always do things in the most practical way.
    I learnt to overcome this by observing others
    and through working with highly pragmatic
    colleagues.

6. **Financial:** resources and opportunities that were
    or were not available
    We are motivated by combinations of different
    things. My motivation is to make a difference
    (cliché as it sounds) by making the world a better
    place. Achieving something meaningful like
    this requires focus, a range of resources and
    opportunities (offered and created). I realised that
    the most important and precious resource I had
    was time.

7. **Vocational:** identifying and doing what only you are on this planet to fulfil

   Writing my first book *The Career Itch* in 2009 gave me a sound approach for realising and fulfilling my vocation. I also took regular retreats, which gave me quality time and a space to think about what I offer and the unique value I bring.

How do you know when the end of the 'becoming-who-you-are' process occurs? For me it was intuitive. I felt that I had 'bottomed out' each of the inner and outer features. I had given myself time (years!) and space to become more comfortable in my own skin. I now had a good idea as to what the next level looked like. That gave me clarity about all the parts of myself: some I would let go of, others would remain and I was ready to welcome in the new.

INTER-AUTHENTICITY

I have described the practical things I did to get to know myself, stay true to myself, express myself and accept myself. The numerous conversations I had with others were particularly insightful. Why? Voicing my leadership stories accelerated my self-awareness; I better understood how the inner and outer features were intermingling.

Storytelling is possibly the most powerful and effective way to exchange knowledge. When we share who we were being, what we were thinking, saying and doing we step back from ourselves as if looking in a mirror. When we share and hear others stories we cannot help but see ourselves through others.

We need each other's leadership stories – the positive, difficult and unresolved – because these reveal the real challenges of leadership. If we shy away from these, we will always be frustrated thinking that leadership should not be like this. Disappointment can lead to demotivation, which in turn negatively affects our performance and relationships in the domains where we lead.

This idea of storytelling is akin to what Desmond Tutu calls *UBUNTU*, a southern and central African word that means all humanity is connected through a universal bond of sharing. Tutu says that a person is a person through another person, that his or her humanity is caught up, bound up inextricably, with yours. We must remember that leaders are human beings first.

I have only made it this far because of others' stories. They have influenced and guided me towards authenticity. I have become who I am because of other leaders.

ACTIONS TO TAKE

I hope you responded to the questions as you read through this chapter. Before we go on you may want to re-read your responses. Now you are going to have a chance to take a deeper look at who you are becoming.

Do not be afraid to look at yourself and see who you really are. These actions are not about nit-picking or self-flagellation. You are not being tested or judged as if taking part in some leadership beauty competition. I know first-hand how hard it is to keep taking an honest look at the inner and outer parts of yourself, particularly if you do not like what you see.

Schedule time in your diary and complete the following activities in sequence because one leads on to another.

Who do you think you are becoming?

Rank each of the features of the inner you and outer you from pages 71 to 72 on a scale of one to ten, from little importance to high importance. What does this ranking suggest to you?

Which one of the features resonates with you most of all? Write a paragraph about it and re-read the paragraph slowly. What does this reveal about who you are becoming?

Which one of the features are you avoiding most? Be courageous and write a paragraph about it and re-read the paragraph slowly. What does this reveal about who you are becoming?

Which one of the features are you most curious about? Hold fifteen-minute interviews with three to six people to gather feedback about how they see this feature in you. Spend longer if they are willing. What similarities and differences are there? Why might this be?

What have you learned about yourself from the leaders' stories in this chapter?

We are all under immense pressure to look like others. So if at first you 'run away', keep coming back and eventually you will begin to like, accept and hopefully embrace who you have been, are being and becoming. In doing this, you will lead in a truly authentic way.

MOVING ON

Are you feeling that authenticity is hard to grasp and achieve? You are right. It requires tenacity to be a You-shaped leader as you make progress at the next level and whenever you hear *The Leader's Call*. There is a great reward for your efforts. Knowing, being, expressing and accepting yourself leads to deeper, more profound relationships and you will have a greater positive impact in the world. Be encouraged!

In this chapter, we have discussed the importance of authenticity. I have shared the process for becoming who you are. You have read how the stories of Ingrid, Ryan, Yolanda and Kim Lee highlighted the four stages.

Every day is an opportunity for you to see more of yourself and to share this when you are leading in the five domains of leadership.

Now it is time to go forward to insight number three, where L is for Learning.

> **'Be yourself, everyone else is taken'**
> Oscar Wilde

INSIGHT

3

is for

LEARNING

> 'Whatever we learn to do,
> we learn by actually doing it'
>
> Aristotle

DEVELOPING MASTERY

Being a committed and authentic leader means that you never stop learning, because learning is central to leading yourself effectively when you are in the domain. *The Leader's Call* moves you to and through levels where you will encounter many different lessons. You need to assess your repertoire of skills and be innovative about plugging any gaps. Your knowledge broadens and deepens.

Please note: mastery will not be achieved by waiting for others to inspire and motivate you. It will feel like a hard slog at times, but whichever domains you lead in you have to take personal responsibility to self-direct your learning. Be willing to participate in learning with others and to personalise your own leader development programme.

You have the potential to go from being a novice leader to a master leader. It will not be easy, but you can achieve this if you are willing to go through a typical and well-

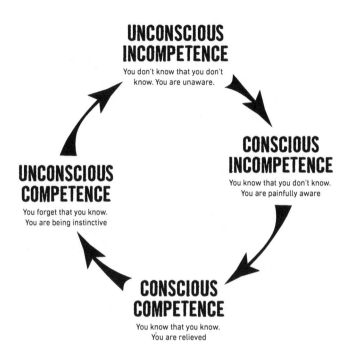

UNCONSCIOUS INCOMPETENCE
You don't know that you don't know. You are unaware.

CONSCIOUS INCOMPETENCE
You know that you don't know. You are painfully aware

UNCONSCIOUS COMPETENCE
You forget that you know. You are being instinctive

CONSCIOUS COMPETENCE
You know that you know. You are relieved

known learning cycle (see above). You will go through the cycle multiple times as you move from one leadership experience to the next, whether you are just starting out or have reached a higher leadership level.

Between conscious incompetence and conscious competence is a very steep learning curve. Remember when you learnt to ride a bike, drive a car, started a team sport, played an instrument or studied a different topic at school? At first it was so difficult and you never thought you would 'get it'. You kept trying, you failed and gave up. You tried again and got upset. Then all of a sudden you noticed tiny improvements. You were happy!

The ancient Greek philosopher, Epictetus said, 'if you

want to improve, be content to be thought foolish'. Learning means you will get some things right and get some things wrong. Interestingly, there are leaders who find it equally difficult to embrace failure and to celebrate success. Learning is bitter sweet. It is through trial and error that you will become a competent leader. Developing mastery is to be perceived as having natural authority and expertise.

I meet leaders who forget they are learning while leading, especially those who have been to and through many levels of leadership experience. They are very hard on themselves and frustrated when they do not know what they believe they *should* know. This results in leaders believing that they are imposters and they are scared about being 'found out'.

Other leaders wonder if they can still learn or learn quickly enough. Some do not know what to learn, which is ironic in these days when we are all seen as knowledge workers. Being a leader is truly a voyage of discovery, whether you are new to it or not.

Being a master leader takes time, but it is not a matter of age or grey hair. It is an art and a science. You learn things in both a spontaneous, unexpected way and a planned, structured way. Master leaders are seen as a 'safe pair of hands'. This is because you have mastered leading yourself, others and functions within organisations and society. Mastery is measured by your proven track record across the five domains.

It is other leaders who will see your mastery. You will realise this when leaders want to know your story; they believe you are credible and connect with your authentic leadership style. They seek your advice, which may turn into a mentoring relationship. Whether you accidentally or deliberately transfer your experiences, skills and knowledge to develop other leaders, it is when you do this consistently that you will have developed mastery.

However, mastery is not a one-stop destination, it is a lifelong (forever!) and subtle process of growth – personally and professionally. Paradoxically, the more you know about being a leader, leading and leadership, the more you realise there is much more to know. This in itself keeps master leaders in a learning mode...and humble!

You will need to know generic things about leadership and specific things that are relevant to your situation. You need to be an active learner, engaging your heart (what you value and believe in), your head (all parts of your brain and mindset) and your hands (experimenting and transferring your knowing into doing). At times you will have to accelerate your learning and at others forcibly slow it down.

In this chapter, we will learn about the elements for 'developing mastery' through other leaders' stories. I will share how I went about self-directing my learning. There are actions to help reinforce and embed all that you come across through this insight. All this is designed to equip you to be more than competent when you respond to *The Leader's Call*. The learning you have done so far is useful but it may not be enough to keep you at the next level. If you continue learning, you will increase your chances.

LEARNING ON THE MOVE

You will encounter learning moments **all** the time but you will not notice them unless you pause. It is like travelling: you need to engage consciously and actively with where you are, whether it is new or familiar territory. Appreciating your surroundings requires you to be present and pay attention to your current situation. When you do this you will learn more effectively.

To pause goes against the grain. Why? Leaders are recognised and rewarded for how they perform and what they produce. If there is too much work to do they tend to do it quickly, thinking their performance will be even better! This is short-sighted because if you miss out on the learning, which the domains have in store for you, you will not develop mastery. Your senses are constantly picking up stimulus and signals from your environment. You become what you learn.

Your learning is made up of four elements:

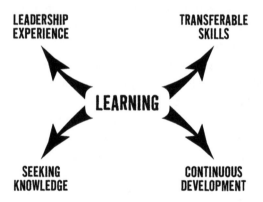

| LEADERSHIP EXPERIENCE | TRANSFERABLE SKILLS |
| SEEKING KNOWLEDGE | CONTINUOUS DEVELOPMENT |

How do these relate to developing mastery? Working through tough, daily leader experiences, instead of resisting them, makes you better able to cope with the uncertainty. Expanding your skills rather than sticking to your usual repertoire will give you the practical agility to deal with complexity in the five domains. Applying what you know to the ambiguous situations you face will make a difference. If you keep developing, you will grow into a mature leader with presence, influence and the ability to develop others.

LEADERSHIP EXPERIENCE
NASIR'S STORY

We met while I was co-facilitating on a leadership programme, which had all types of leaders present (the reluctant, the new, the experienced and mentors). They came from all sectors. These were culturally diverse women and men, who alongside their local, national and global roles had caring responsibilities in and outside their homes.

Their hours ranged from 'officially' working part time to full time (over four days) and full time (over five days) throughout the year while on permanent, interim, rolling and term-time contracts. Some generated further income from hobbies and interests. Others were active volunteers in their communities and professional networks. This was a group of people who were busy, or as Nasir put it 'we are always "on" in this 24/7/365 world'.

When I surveyed the group at the start of the programme most had never had any formal leadership development. For the majority their learning was done, informally, every day on the job and they all related to having been 'consciously incompetent' at times. Each leader had technical or specialist aspects to their roles. The size of their office-based and virtual teams ranged from one to sixty and all operated across different time zones.

Several times during the programme Nasir made comments about how difficult he was finding the experience of being a leader. He was trying to stay up to date with his area of expertise and on top of several projects. Nasir did not feel supported by his line manager and he was exasperated with members in his team. His only enjoyment was the after-work socialising with a small group of peers whom, he told us, he trusted and respected.

What surprised him was that all of the leaders on the programme echoed his comments, to a greater or lesser extent. Although his comments were not new to me, his honesty and vulnerability gave permission for others to say how they really felt. It did not take long before other participants were also exchanging countless examples of their own situation. With their guards dropped they were openly sharing and supporting each other.

When Nasir said, almost to himself, 'I am glad that I'm not alone,' he looked relieved. As I packed up at the end of day one, Nasir offered to help and I sensed that he still had much more to say. He did. Nasir had not yet learnt how to work through the daily pressures of leadership. He had never had this kind of conversation with anyone other than his peers and he was now offloading a psychological burden he had long been carrying.

Tell it like it is

What Nasir and his fellow participants were doing, in a safe learning space, was taking a warts and all look at their leadership experiences. Being away from the maelstrom of working life and stepping back from the daily hustle and bustle can have an interesting effect. Suppressed feelings, thoughts and opinions come up to the surface; these will be expressed with no holds barred if there is trust and solidarity.

The group's comments were, in my view, natural, important and very healthy. I would rather leaders said what is really going on, from their perspective, than pretend all is well. It is better to empty out what they are carrying around in their hearts and heads, rather than have it take up valuable mental space and energy. When leaders share openly, learning is accelerated for all. How? They become more competent when exploring real dilemmas.

While this may, on the surface, sound like whingeing or over-indulgence to those who find it uncomfortable to hear such disclosures, it is not. Consider if leaders are unable to voice these frustrations and work through issues with other leaders – they will not learn how to manage their own expectations and cope with deeply unsettling uncertainty.

Leaders should not retreat from the challenges, give up or blame others for what is 'going wrong'. They learn when, rather than pointing their finger at others, they ask themselves what part they can play to influence or change the situation. If you decide, despite all you have to offer, to leave (or run away) from the 'messy' domains your absence will be a big loss to those around you and the levels ahead.

At the end of the leadership development programme Nasir and the other leaders shared what they had learned about themselves, others and the five domains of leadership. He admitted that his frustration had lessened because of new techniques he had acquired. For him the most important thing of all was having a group of peers that he could talk to in future.

This story demonstrates that everyone learns when leaders can freely and truthfully air their experiences with peers in a safe and supportive learning environment. There will be times when leaders feel overwhelmed and burdened by their leadership responsibilities. Having inadequate support and space to share is akin to leaders and their teams being set up to fail.

Nasir realised, that instead of fearing and being in denial of the leader experiences that come his way, the best response is to make choices that empower him to face them head on. If you take personal responsibility to learn through facing your own challenges you will become more and more resilient. You will be surprised at what you can extract from all your leadership experiences, positive or negative. They contain many lessons.

Now let us take a closer look at some of the different things leaders have to contend with in their professional and personal lives.

The everyday life of a leader

For a leader, there are demanding tasks to juggle and deliver against competing timescales. There are systems you need to create and maintain 'behind the scenes'. There are people you meet across cultural boundaries with different personalities and leadership styles, and whose combined assumptions, interests, priorities, objectives and expectations can often generate misunderstanding and conflict. Is it any wonder that being a leader can be so tough?

Each day leaders are responsible and accountable for a range of different things, which I see falling into three categories: tasks, administration and people. I have included some examples from my own 'in tray' relating to my business and family for the coming month.

FROM GRACE'S 'IN TRAY'

Tasks

(doing or assigning a piece of work within a given timeframe)

Solution preparation, design and delivery, attending meetings (face-to-face/virtual), planning, organising, communicating, liaising, reading, event management, researching, writing, giving and receiving feedback, relationship building, crisis management

---

Administration

(systems and processes for effectiveness and efficiency)

Diary management, emails, attending to and filing paperwork (virtual and physical), travel arrangements, expenses and making payments, responding to messages by phone, text and via social media platforms!

People

(those you are connected to and who have an interest in what you do)

Yourself, family members, line manager/s, direct reports, teams, peers, other colleagues, clients, partners, suppliers, customers, neighbours, the general public, investors, civil servants

Make notes about what is going on for you now, this week, month, quarter or year!

Tasks

(doing or assigning a piece of work within a given timeframe)

Administration

(systems and processes for effectiveness and efficiency)

People

(those you are connected to and who have an interest in what you do)

Often we do not fully appreciate what we are actually doing until we write it down. Each item looks straightforward, but on breaking them down we find they are complex and multi-dimensional; some are perhaps out of our direct control which can lead to frustration.

These three categories and the examples show that leaders are under pressure to do what they are employed (or have volunteered) to do while at the same time lead their (inner and outer) selves well. The amount of time and energy utilised by tasks, administration and people varies daily and throughout your leadership experience. Do not expect it always to be the same.

There are many lessons in the examples I have shared and it is probably the same with the examples you have noted. However, it would be overwhelming to attempt to learn from all of them.

Therefore, in the next activity, choose one example from each category this week and ask questions such as 'what have I learned?' and 'what will I stop, start and continue doing?' This activity can take fifteen to thirty minutes at the start, middle or end of the week. You will be amazed by how much you have been learning subconsciously.

Select one example from each of your lists and make a note on page 115 of the lessons you have learnt from considering them and then what actions you will take.

I have given you an example of mine on page 114.

GRACE LEARNS!

- **Tasks**

  I have learnt that there are times when virtual meetings can be more appropriate and less time consuming than face-to-face meetings. *I will stop* assuming that I always have to meet face to face with clients. *I will start* offering virtual meetings as an option. *I will continue* to ensure that every meeting is timed and that it has a clear agenda.

- **Administration**

  I have learnt that my diary management is becoming more complicated as the number of opportunities increases. *I will stop* being (or try not being) overly stressed by this. *I will start* a weekly review of the opportunities so that I know where I am with each. *I will continue* to excel at planning and organising!

- **People**

  I have learnt (again) that *I am unable* to communicate with all my stakeholders all of the time. *I will stop* attempting to do this and start to re-prioritise those *I can stay* in contact with. *I will continue* delegating other contacts to my virtual assistant .

Now it is your turn.

.... LEARNS!

(insert your name)

- **Tasks**

  I have learnt that...

  I will stop...

  I will start...

  I will continue...

- **Administration**

  I have learnt that...

  I will stop...

  I will start...

  I will continue...

- **People**

  I have learnt that...

  I will stop...

  I will start...

  I will continue...

At your next leadership level the number of tasks will increase. The systems and processes in place will need to be reviewed to cope with the growth in your workload. You will meet more people like you and unlike you. All this will challenge how you relate to others.

As a leader these categories are where your time goes. When there is so much to get done, it is easy to underestimate and undervalue what you are learning as you go about each day. Whatever environment you lead in – it is your classroom. Start learning!

TRANSFERABLE SKILLS

MADDIE'S STORY

She was known for being very talented in her area of expertise and responding to The Leader's Call meant starting a business. She outsourced as much administration as possible to a team of virtual assistants because it was not 'her thing' and she wanted to focus on what she was really good at: generating ideas, delivering projects and building relationships with people, her team, suppliers and clients.

I had mentored one of her friends and through word of mouth Maddie and I started working together. It had taken her years to accept that she was a leader. She had associated the word with negative connations due to her bad experiences with incompetent leaders. As a result she had put limits on her potential.

Maddie uncovered these deep-seated, limiting beliefs when she had been asked during a leadership seminar to complete a beliefs association exercise. She spent one minute writing down all the beliefs that she associated with being a leader. Looking through them she realised the majority were negative. She suspected they could not all be true! This was the revelation she needed to admit and accept that she was a leader. Now Maddie wanted to take responsibility for being the best leader that she could be.

She told me, 'I want to identify, assess and communicate my leadership skills better. This is one of my goals for the financial year.' Now that her business had a 'bread and butter' source of income and a pipeline of work she wanted to spend time developing her leadership potential and she diarised two hours a week to do this.

Back to basics

During one of our conversations I explained to Maddie that because she (and other leaders) had literally hundreds of skills, it would take a very long time to identify them all individually. While I could offer her a generic list of leadership skills it would not enable her to identify and assess those specific to her own experiences.

We agreed her starting point should be to group and then assess her own leadership skills. Following that, we could address her need to keep a regular track of her skills development and acquisition. Maddie hired a brand consultant to lay out and present information to ensure her outer self was consistent across all communication media. The hard bit (which she admitted to avoiding as she felt it would 'be so tedious'), was gathering the content – and no one could do that except Maddie!

The leadership skills groups we agreed on were technical (areas of expertise), operational (day-to-day management) and interpersonal (relating to others). These three featured prominently in her daily leadership experiences. To capture how she had demonstrated these over a longer time frame, she drew a timeline of her leadership experiences (those she could recall), which spanned decades. She then recorded on paper all her roles (professional and personal) along with key high points, low points and turning points.

Using the three groups she listed under each the skills that she had used or developed at each point in time. To jog her memory, Maddie downloaded skill lists from the internet and highlighted those that related to her roles as a parent, in employment, as a business owner and a volunteer. This task took her three months to complete. By the end she had identified thirty skills in each of the groups. She admitted to having enjoyed it!

Maddie was thrilled and excited to discover the skills she saw in herself. These included skills that others had told her she had (though she had not believed them till now) and skills she had not known she possessed. However, it was impractical for Maddie to present all ninety skills to the outside world. It would be best to reduce the list to core skills, around ten in each group.

As she had recently entered the next level we agreed it would be useful to include other people related to her different roles to gain valuable feedback. Having done the initial work of identification, she hoped that these others would challenge and support her self-diagnosis and assessment.

Into the five domains
To make this potentially daunting task more manageable, she selected twenty people from her family, team, peers, suppliers, clients, past employers and community

volunteers. They would assess the skills, provide specific examples of these in action and recommend how she could further improve as a leader in these skills areas.

To achieve a level of objectivity she asked a virtual assistant to set up an online survey with the assessment plus questions for each member of her network to complete. The assistant contacted each person with a personalised email and survey link. After a month Maddie had a report with the compiled responses. We met again to discuss the findings.

She was moved and overwhelmed (in a good way) by the generosity and honesty of the comments, especially those from her nearest and dearest who saw her at her most vulnerable moments. What amazed her most was how a small number of skills kept being referred to – it became apparent that these were at her core.

If Maddie had only evaluated on her own, she would have missed out on this opportunity to learn how others perceived her and to realise her leadership potential yet to be released. Developing mastery requires you to be self-aware and seek out feedback from others.

Now that she had a skills baseline, Maddie decided to complete a similar feedback exercise bi-annually. This way she could stay on track with her leadership skills development and acquisition, then regularly update her external profile information.

This entire process gave Maddie the confidence to communicate three skills from each group in her CV, on brand materials and across her social media platforms. She had achieved all this well within her deadline.

ASSESS YOUR LEADERSHIP SKILLS

You may not have time to create a list of all your leadership skills. While I believe that a personalised approach to your skills assessment is more authentic and meaningful, I do realise that we all have to start somewhere. Whether you are leading as a parent, carer, business owner, employee or volunteer there are a range of online and offline resources that can help you to identify, assess, develop and communicate your leadership skills.

In my time of designing, delivering, evaluating and participating in more than forty leadership programmes, I have found these to be the core skill groups. Each has examples of what these skills look like in practice and I have drawn upon the five intelligences (intellectual, emotional, political (in an organisation sense), cultural, spiritual) to create them.

Rate your level of ability on a scale of one to four where:

4 = Highly able   Others see you as a mentor

3 = Able   You have a proven track record

2 = Developing   You feel consciously incompetent

1 = Unable   You feel this might be a development need

Once you have completed the skills assessment, you may want, as Maddie did, to ask others in your network for their feedback. I wonder what you will learn.

continued...

TECHNICAL – AREAS OF EXPERTISE

RATING

Aware of current trends and developments
in the field

Connected to people who are further ahead
in technical mastery

Making complex information simple
and accessible

Drive to deliver consistently high quality solutions

Recall theories, models and examples
when required

Time out for continuous professional development

Using a range of creative approaches and media

Reflecting on successes and failure of yourself
and others

Minimising reputational damage through
ethical practice

Seeking out alternative perspectives to
challenge perception

Total score out of 40

What might this tell you about your technical skills?

continued...

OPERATIONAL – DAY-TO-DAY MANAGEMENT

Managing conflicting priorities and adapting
to unexpected issues

Delegating tasks to team members effectively
and respectfully

Being responsive to queries and requests

Effective use of resources eg talent, money,
information

Returning to the big picture and keeping the
vision in sight

Fostering a positive attitude in the working
environment

Training, coaching and mentoring team members

Reviewing, monitoring and evaluating performance

Delivering to deadlines and targets while managing
expectations

Critical thinking to solve problems, make decisions
and contingencies

Total score out of 40

What might this tell you about your operational skills?

continued...

INTERPERSONAL – RELATING TO OTHERS

RATING

Listening attentively and openly to all types of people

Modelling authenticity whoever the 'audience' is

Developing, nurturing and maintaining trust

Regularly seeking and giving quality feedback

Ability to discern, affirm, inspire and collaborate

Using your presence and energy to empower others

Communicating through a range of media, face to face and virtually

Sensing dynamics, power and politics without being intimidated

Building a network of genuine, diverse relationships

Addressing conflict, dysfunction and incongruent behaviour

Total score out of 40

What might this tell you about your interpersonal skills?

SEEKING KNOWLEDGE

ERIN'S STORY

It was a passion for and a commitment to learning that connected us. When we shared our leadership experiences we discovered similarities and differences. Over time we became sounding boards for each other. Our areas of expertise were complementary and while I tended to work independently, Erin was a senior leader for an international organisation.

During one of our meet ups Erin mentioned that an opportunity to move to the next level had come about even though she had not anticipated it. She was not sure if she wanted to consider it but that if she did the opportunity would require her to do less in her area of expertise and more in the area of leading a cross-cultural virtual team.

Erin loved being an expert. Before making a personally and professionally life-changing decision, she wanted to explore what she might be letting herself in for. Other senior leaders she had known with similar levels of expertise found the people bit of their role the most challenging. Over time some became good at it but others gave up because they struggled to do the technical, operational and interpersonal parts well.

Having gone online to research the topic 'leading people', Erin was stunned by the amount of information out there. Going to a local bookshop was just as overwhelming with tomes of books that would take her years to read, let alone understand! 'Where do I start?', she asked me, knowing that this was an area of my expertise. 'I only have eight weeks to learn about what I know that I don't know.'

Start from where you are

The thing about knowledge is that there is so much of it out there! Finding what meets your need can be like looking for a needle in a haystack. I suspect that much of the knowledge out there is 'nice to know' versus what you 'need to know'.

With only an eight-week timeframe, Erin narrowed down the leadership topic of her enquiry. During a conversation she decided that 'leading people' was too broad a term and that what she really needed to know about was 'leading a cross-cultural virtual team effectively'.

As we talked through how she could identify the knowledge sources Erin decided that turning her search into an open question would enable her to take a more curious approach instead of looking for an absolute answer. Her question was 'how do I lead a cross-cultural virtual team effectively?'

Having defined the question, we discussed possible knowledge sources that could give her an insight into the everyday realities of leading a cross-cultural virtual team effectively. She had perused the leading theories and models, some of which appeared contradictory. What she wanted to know about was what she could apply immediately in the role.

Erin made the assumption that she did not have any relevant knowledge despite her senior leadership experience. I encouraged her to see herself as a potential source of knowledge because, like skills, our knowledge is also transferable. She had not thought about reflecting on her own experiences of leading teams but agreed to this, again out of curiosity.

We ended up with three knowledge sources:

- **First hand** – Erin's self-reflection
- **Second hand** – talking to leaders from her network
- **Third hand** – online research and resources at work

Erin did not have lots of spare time over the eight weeks so she allocated one hour a week. As we discussed this Erin realised what she really wanted were different perspectives and help in unravelling a potentially complex topic. Eight hours, she decided, was a good start and better than having no time at all.

She was amazed at how much it was possible to get done with a focused approach. Erin told me that if we had not worked together she would not have had the clarity needed to acquire the specific knowledge to help her make a very important decision. Our working approach enabled her to minimise the distractions (especially during the online search) and focus on what she needed to know.

Just-in-time knowledge

We met to discuss her learning and the answers to her question about leading a cross-cultural virtual team effectively.

Erin was pleasantly surprised at how much she had learned and the answers she had found to her question. As we talked everything through and as she wrote things down, she realised the breadth and depth of her existing knowledge plus that which was newly acquired.

On the back of this enquiry she had a much better idea and picture of what would be expected of her and

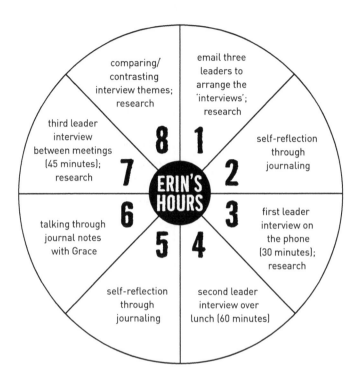

HOW ERIN ALLOCATED HER EIGHT HOURS

also the benefits and pitfalls of the role. Erin decided to take up this new role because it was her next level; but not before agreeing with her employer to put support structures in place to aid a smooth transition from her existing level.

The support structures included regular contact with her line manager, continuing to work with me through the first hundred days of the new role, meeting with the three original leader interviewees over lunch and after work to talk through their individual and shared issues and successes (they eventually formed a peer development

ERIN'S RESEARCH	FIRST HAND Erin's self-reflection
What she learnt	In my job roles I have led teams through common sense, intuition and on-the-job experience rather than tried and tested approaches. I seek to work with team members equally no matter their age or background.
Actions to take	Having confidence in my own experiences; I know more than I realise. Revisit feedback from past team members about what did work, what didn't work and what I can do differently in future. Respond to situations accordingly.

SECOND HAND
Talking to leaders from her network

THIRD HAND
Research online and her employer's resources

The purpose of my role is to help the team flourish while delivering the strategy. I do this by creating the conditions for high performance through regular, quality one-to-one and team conversations. Prioritise time with each team member and observe the dynamics when they interact together.

Be brave, address conflict and underperformance as soon as possible. Have fun together! Through a short podcast, video and book extract she learnt that every team has its own subculture; there are always reasons for dysfunction, lack of trust, cohesion and harmony. Time out for assessing individual and collective performance with a facilitator will give us all insights into how things are progressing and what needs to stop, start and continue so that we can all succeed.

Communicating with the team on a regular basis is essential so that I can learn about them as individuals and their talents, not as a collective. We need to agree etiquette around virtual ways of working. My role is to stay connected with key stakeholders and parts of the organisation so that I can champion the team, maintain our visibility and influence those with a vested interest.

There is much more to know! Cross-cultural virtual teams are challenging because of heterogeneity, time zones, calendar variations and real or imagined boundaries. They are more interesting because of personal styles and cultural stereotypes/ overlaps. They can be rewarding if I remain aware of my own cultural influences and open to doing things in a more creative and flexible way.

group). She was successful in negotiating a small budget for resources to aid her ongoing development in the role.

When you want to refresh your knowledge or understand a new topic your immediate response may be registering for a short course, attempting to read a tome or going on an expensive programme. If you react in this way, try reflecting on your experiences first. Then talk to those who have been to where you are going. Afterwards do some online/offline research – you will find bite-sized information as well as three-course meals!

Leading yourself at the next level means taking control of how and when you learn.

CONTINUOUS DEVELOPMENT

ZARA'S STORY

As we neared the end of a pro bono mentoring programme Zara wanted to take a more planned approach to her leader development. We started working together because she felt almost paralysed by the feeling of conscious incompetence in her voluntary work with a community-based arts and culture organisation. Usually positive and resilient Zara had been taken aback at how fearful she had become. She did not recognise herself.

Working as a volunteer in this new enterprise meant the usual structures and processes that she was accustomed to in her paid work were not in place. This made her feel insecure. Income for the work was ad hoc. She sensed odd dynamics in the environment. Forming harmonious relationships was challenging due to diverse working patterns and varying levels of commitment. Stakeholders were inaccessible because of their other priorities.

Zara had simply wanted to offer her leadership experience, skills and knowledge to a fast-growing community enterprise whose values she shared. With hindsight she had made big assumptions about what she needed to do to be effective. She imagined how to do the role, how to communicate and how to take the team along with her.

She found after the first week that her mental bubble of inspiration had burst. Zara felt out of control and frustrated. What had seemed like a straightforward task was turning into something deeply confusing and difficult.

Over a nine-month period she moved closer to feeling consciously competent and had regained her upbeat personality. The big lesson for her was recognising that a strong skill in analysing situations had almost derailed her performance because the fear led her to become over analytical and critical of herself and others involved.

The quantum leap came when Zara had been reading about the neuroscience of learning. She came to understand that her brain had been hardwired over time through the repetitive nature of her paid work. She excelled at certain things and this made it more difficult to adapt, which is what she needed to do in this role. Hope for her came when she read the evidence that every human being has capacity to change, if they choose to.

Through our mentoring conversations her brain had literally changed. Her mindset had shifted from being the expert to being the expert-novice. This is because there were things she could offer, which the community organisation desperately needed. However, she was also on a steep learning curve. She accepted each lesson with humility and gratitude.

YOUR MASTERY PLAN

To develop mastery, you will need to capture the spontaneous lessons of your leadership experience wherever you are. Of course there will be times when your development will be organised and planned in advance. You will set out to reinforce and acquire the skills and the knowledge that you need to perform your roles competently at the next level.

Find a way to recall, record and reflect frequently on what you have learnt, are learning and plan to learn. Doing this will transform you into a master leader.

Zara and I co-created this simple template (opposite) that she could fill in at the end of each month before our sessions. This 'homework' enabled her to pause, step back and critically examine her inner and outer self to capture what might have gone unnoticed and what was unforgettable.

This new habit took real commitment and because the benefits far outweighed the effort Zara kept going, even after our mentoring arrangement came to an end. She gained so many insights through completing her plan. These gently nudged her towards behaving in a way which was authentic and she wanted to model to others.

You may find a template like this to be of use, you may have another or you may, after reading this chapter, design your own. The format or template does not matter.

In time your mastery plan has the potential to help you to experience smoother transitions through the steep learning curve. It will still be a challenge but you will feel less fearful and more in control. All that remains is for you to transfer your learning, so that what you now 'know'

QUESTIONS	NOTES ABOUT THE SITUATION
1. What happened?	
2. How did it make me feel, think and behave? Why might that be?	
3. What did I learn about myself, others and the situation? How is this useful to me and others?	
4. What skills did I use/ develop? (technical, operational, interpersonal)	
5. What knowledge have I acquired/shared? (self-reflection, others, research)	
6. What action/s will I take? When? Who can hold me accountable? Do I need resources? Where are they?	

you can 'do'. Applying what you have become aware of will mean that you will lead yourself effectively across the five domains and generate an even more positive impact.

DIRECT YOUR LEARNING

I love to learn in different ways and believe in learning through all the senses. Being a committed life-long learner I have developed a learning mindset over decades. Each year I seek out new experiences, transfer my skills and acquire knowledge. I also curate and facilitate learning for others, in organisations, teams, groups and one to one. So how do I go about self-directing and personalising my learning? Here are some examples.

- Spending one day in each season on a retreat where I can reflect on my life and leadership experiences in a quiet, safe and inspirational space. Sometimes I take things to read or listen to. At other times I meet strangers there and we have interesting conversations about local, national and global issues. I take my journal so that I can write, draw models and doodle. I always learn something from these restorative times.

- I review my skill abilities and gaps through well-known and little-known self-assessments. If there are reports, I peruse and analyse them with curiosity, understanding that they are snapshots of the leader I am at that time. The assessments can be tens of pounds, others are free. I always learn something from the feedback.

- I save blogs, articles and reports about being a leader, leading and leadership in a learning e-folder. I come back to it every couple of weeks and after going through it I file the knowledge I find most interesting into a research file and my toolkit. I attend talks, events and conferences. I listen to podcasts, the radio and log on to webinars (web-based seminars). I watch videos online and programmes on television. I always learn something.

- A friend and I go on trips to arts and culture events and venues where we eat and talk and watch creative masters at work. While enjoying these experiences I have many 'a-ha' moments. Clarity arrives after I have been trying to work something out for weeks. I always learn something in this playtime.

- I also have mentors and peer supervisors, and have leadership role models (alive and dead), whose stories I find inspiring and informative.

All of this (and more) amounts to my hybrid-style, leader development programme.

PRACTICE MAKES PERMANENT

Writing this chapter has been poignant for me. I have been reminded how far I have come in my own development as a human being and woman with multiple leader roles. From starting out as netball captain through to being considered a master by other leaders (which I admit I do not always see). Why? In my bid to stay focused on the present and future I do not keep revisiting all I have done (there is a lot to trawl through) and often forget what I have achieved...

However, I do recognise, accept and celebrate that just like the proverbial Russian dolls I have grown up and my character has matured (still a way to go!) through many different leadership experiences. As time has gone on my confidence has improved as has my competence.

As we grow as leaders, we learn and relearn so that we can flourish in the five domains. It is easy to forget that with each move to the next level most of what we learn continues to be held within us, just as each Russian doll sits in the other. Your learning may be hidden and tucked away from view but it is there for you to draw on; it resides there for all the years to come.

ACTIONS TO TAKE

Whatever your learning style and preferences, there are lessons waiting for you to learn consciously and subconsciously. You are a leader in progress and developing mastery is not about becoming a perfect role model. It means that you are ready and willing to learn from all that comes at and to you – the good, the bad and surprising!

If you have completed some or all of the activities in this chapter, you will be more aware of how much you can learn by paying close attention to what is going on within and around you. If there are specific areas that you want to follow up on, great! I also encourage you to complete the activities on the pages 138 to 139. All this is part of your mastery plan.

SWIM, DON'T SINK

Learning through experience, skills, knowledge and development is not about dipping your toes in the water – you have to jump or dive in. Being a leader means taking calculated risks. In this way you will get used to the leadership environment you are in without becoming institutionalised and constrained by the status quo.

Whether your preference is for learning that is short or for a long-term learning programme or somewhere in between, the choice is yours. You can be single minded and selective or open minded and expansive when it comes to self-directing your learning and fulfilling your mastery plan. Learning must be relevant and timely for you.

Being a leader is deeply personal and a developmental process that happens over years. With each cycle of change and transition that comes at the next level you will attract greater responsibilities and unexpected challenges. The five domains present you with an array of lessons and through them you will grow and mature... if you choose to.

MOVING ON

Whether you are hovering at the start, in the middle of or are reaching the threshold of the next level, learning all the way is imperative. Like any craftsperson honing a skill, mastery does not happen overnight. Mastery is not about bolstering your ego or feeling good about yourself (though you might). Modesty is needed so that you are able to pass on your experience, skills and knowledge to others – they are learning and so are you. In doing this you will equip other leaders to become competent, confident and consistent.

LEADERSHIP EXPERIENCE

When you are inspired or bothered by a situation, it usually means that it is a learning moment for you. To capture what happened write a few paragraphs about it. Then re-read your notes and make any changes. Afterwards consider what this situation can teach you about yourself and others. Make a note of your insights.

....
....
....
....
....

TRANSFERABLE SKILLS

Complete all or one of the skills assessments on pages 121 to 123. What can you do to fill your skills gaps within the technical, operational or interpersonal areas?

....
....
....
....
....
....
....
....

SEEKING KNOWLEDGE

What leadership topics are an issue or of interest?
What might you need to know about in order to be more
effective? What are the sources of this knowledge?

....
....
....
....
....
....
....
....
....
....

CONTINUOUS DEVELOPMENT

Create your own mastery plan or try Zara's and use it
over a four-week timeframe to capture what you are
learning. What behaviours are you modelling?

....
....
....
....
....
....
....
....
....
....

Your role as a master leader is to empower other leaders to develop mastery.

In this chapter, we have learned about the elements for developing mastery through the stories of leaders. I have shared how I went about self-directing my learning. Keep on learning and you are guaranteed to survive and thrive when you hear *The Leader's Call*.

We are almost at the end of this book, with the fourth and final insight coming up next, where L is for Legacy. Keep going, you are nearly there. Onwards!

'Learn from everything'

Laura Weinblatt

INSIGHT

L
is for
LEGACY

'Strive not to be a success,
but rather to be of value'

Albert Einstein

SUSTAINING YOUR CONTRIBUTION

Legacy is not only for political leaders of countries or
the celebrities that adorn our media channels. We do not
have to wait for anniversaries, attend memorials, read
obituaries or celebrate the beginning of a new century
to start thinking about legacy. Every human being leaves
something behind, by accident or on purpose.

As a leader you have the potential to create a meaningful
legacy. This is a key of part of what it means to be an
effective leader in the twenty-first century. However,
in order to do that you need to be able to sustain your
contribution. What does this mean in practice?

In effect, it is about taking care of your whole self,
staying motivated, keeping on track and passing on your
experience and resources to others. Doing this means your
leadership mark will remain well after you have left. Most
important of all it means that you can make a consistent
contribution wherever you lead, however long that may be.

At the next level leaders make things happen on a small and big scale. This is how, I believe, leaders create value in the five domains of leadership. They turn ideas into reality, transforming whatever they become involved in. Leaders make an impact, generate opportunities, enhance outcomes and leave a positive imprint.

Responding to *The Leader's Call* means you are making a contribution through your unique abilities, which are developed and honed as you lead. These abilities are so valuable because without leaders the status quo remains. Without leaders we would never imagine or believe that the impossible is possible. If, like me, you want to see a better world today and for the next generation – our children, nieces, nephews and godchildren – then we need to look out for and develop more effective leaders.

Months after I heard *The Leader's Call* the Olympics came to London in 2012. Going to the Olympics was on my bucket list so when our family secured tickets for opening day in the stadium, we were ecstatic, to say the least. It was a thrill to sit rows away from the poster girls and boys who had promoted the Games. Despite the sun, rain *and* wind, being a part of that huge crowd while enjoying sport at the highest level is forever etched in my memory. Residing in one of the Olympic boroughs meant that I heard about legacy, a lot!

Legacy is a word readily associated with the Olympics. There was such major concern about what would be left behind once the athletes, spectators and personnel had left, that several committees were set up. These legacy committees operated before, during and after the Olympics to maximise whatever remained. They looked at, for example, financial investment, infrastructure and venues so that local people, the nation and the next generation of athletes might benefit.

So, with the Olympics still fresh in our collective minds, I was asked by the borough where I live to give a talk during October 2012, titled 'The Legacy of Independence'. In the UK, October is when we celebrate Black History Month to keep alive the memory of women, men and children who have left legacies. As I prepared for this talk, I revisited painful and inspiring stories about people of African and Caribbean descent in the UK and overseas.

Some of these stories were familiar to me and others were new discoveries. At various times during his life my father told me about these ancestors, but I had never consciously thought about the legacy that they left visibly and invisibly. He told me about why they shared their talents and took big risks. Many made the ultimate sacrifice, giving their lives to secure freedom and a better life for their loved ones and those following after them.

While interacting with the audience during the talk, I was struck by the importance of not only remembering those who had gone before us but also of replicating the same passion, leadership and spirit of endeavour in those who were alive and those following. It took me two years, after the 'moment' I had on the road in Accra, West Africa, to discern a practical solution to how I could contribute to my country.

I was motivated to start African Diaspora Kids, a legacy community project that connects children in the UK to the beautiful continent of Africa. The mission is to work with families and children aged five to eleven, with educators, supporters and partners to develop the next generation of African Diaspora leaders by 2040. The vision of African

Diaspora Kids is that these children will have created a better life for themselves and their families. They will be active citizens, innovators and philanthropists who occupy significant positions of leadership throughout British society and across the world.

Legacy is not only something that is left after you depart. It is the value, the benefit you are creating and the effort you are multiplying here and now, wherever you are leading.

Being a leader means that you are expanding your contribution in the world. You might inherit legacy in the form of stories and archive material. You take whatever is handed to you by your predecessors. You will inherit systems, processes and teams. Whether your leadership tenure is short or long others will inherit the value that you create. What will other people say about you, about the value you pass on?

This fourth and final insight is concerned with how you sustain the contribution you make, the value you create and the legacy you leave. How can you leverage your abilities and multiply the positive impact in the domains where you lead? How can you identify and look into your blind spots, and minimise derailment? How can you purposefully shape and safeguard your legacy so that whatever you leave for others will empower generations to come?

In this chapter you will find out how leaders grappled with these questions and found answers. I will share what I consider to be important aspects for sustaining your contribution. As usual there are actions at the end. All this is designed to encourage you to think beyond your roles to the bigger picture when you respond to *The Leader's Call*.

THE POWER OF ONE LEADER

A single leader has an immeasurable amount of influence and potential though we do not always recognise or embrace this. We habitually look to and at other leaders to learn from them or we aspire to be like them. It is natural to glance or stare at those beside, in front, above and behind us; but do not underestimate your value. No one can lead in the way you do – remember your uniqueness. You are as much a gift to others as others are to you.

What will it take for you to sustain your contribution and be consistent while you lead? There are four aspects.

SOURCING ENERGY · HAVING AMBITION · KEEPING PERSPECTIVE · PRACTISING GENEROSITY

Read on to see how they play out in the real world of leadership.

SOURCING ENERGY

VERNE'S STORY

We met at the local Pilates class. When I told Verne about my work developing leaders she explained that the reason she did Pilates was because she could not switch off emotionally and mentally from her day job. She had recently been promoted to the board, as one of six directors of a medium-sized organisation that had a global presence.

Verne was driven and enjoyed her role. She talked passionately about the positive difference her employer was making in the world. She said 'I totally underestimated how busy I'd become. Before I started this role no one explained what it would be like at this level. I am a self-confessed workaholic and I get a huge buzz from the work. However, the pressure and stress is taking its toll and I lack the energy I need to keep going.'

Verne had tried all sorts of ways to stay energised. She listed the high impact sports activities she had signed up for, but on arriving at the gym she was too exhausted to give them her all. She went jogging but found it boring because she did not have a specific goal to achieve. Walking her dogs was something she loved because she felt energised while being in nature, but it was often dark when she arrived home from the office.

As we worked together her goal was to identify a pick and mix of options to boost her energy and maintain her wellbeing irrespective of her schedule. She felt this would stop her feeling guilty and depressed about not being able to stick to a regular routine. Most important of all, she told me, was to identify natural energy sources so that she would not become dependent on artificial energy drinks, stimulants or over-the-counter drugs.

She asked to meet with me for a few sessions in order to devise a realistic and flexible plan to increase and maintain her energy levels. Verne said 'I draw energy from the usual things like eating, drinking and movement; these are vital. However, it is more than that. My energy comes from my emotional, mental, spiritual and physical state.'

Putting yourself first

Before our first session, Verne took a week's holiday. It was an emergency measure because she could not sleep at night and her exhaustion felt more like burnout. She had reached her breaking point. It transpired that she had not had a proper break between her former and current role. She had had no time to 'down her tools' and chill out. She had prioritised the new role over her wellbeing and it was proving to be a costly mistake.

On holiday, Verne slept and sat mostly in one place on the beach, doing very little. The fresh air, white clouds, warm sunshine, soft sand and deep blue sea was a much needed change of scenery. During this time, she began to think deeply about what was depleting her energy levels. She put most of it down to her own behaviour, which resulted in her 'running on empty'. Verne wrote a long list of her behaviours; the following were her top ten.

1. Feeling powerless because I am consciously incompetent in the new role
2. Not booking short breaks or holidays
3. Being unwilling to say no and so always feeling 'on'
4. Not asking for help when I desperately need it
5. Being accessible due to a lack of boundaries
6. Staying late at work which means I cannot walk the dogs
7. Failure to delegate to the team because I fear losing control
8. No socialising outside of working relationships
9. Reacting to crises and never getting to the important tasks

10. Fear of not keeping up with others,
    so overworking

Verne was honest with herself. This restorative space away from the office enabled her to notice what was really going on within and outside her. While being in nature she had an epiphany: nature was her primary energy source and her solace. It made her feel good about herself, her life and work. Verne felt that she **had** to be in nature at least twice a week to keep her energy levels up. She returned to work determined to make and sustain the changes.

Staying connected to the source

Prior to our first session Verne emailed me a list of the ten behaviours she wanted help turning into new habits while at the next level. She felt that if she could do these things consistently over the following months she would be able to stay energised for the longer term. Then she would have strategies in place for when *The Leader's Call* came; she did not want to miss out on future opportunities because of her present conduct.

This was her list of new habits.

1. Take responsibility for my behaviour
2. Spend time in nature with the dogs
3. Identify restorative spaces near work
   e.g. gardens and parks
4. Write a work strategy to ruthlessly
   prioritise tasks
5. Delegate to the team and share decision making
6. Book spa weekend retreats every three months

7. Challenge the culture of busyness at work
8. Negotiate to work from home one or two days a week
9. Arrange for an annual health check through work
10. Hire a coach to create a lifestyle plan for this year

Verne had discovered her energy sources and she knew that staying connected to them would enable her to face whatever came at and to her in the domains. During our last conversation she was optimistic and realistic about what was possible. She no longer expected her environment to change – *she* changed and she was reaping the benefits. Now that Verne could switch off when she got home the dogs were always happy to see her!

When the going gets tough

At its worst the five domains of leadership will take you to and beyond your limits, the experience could even turn your hair grey! The domains can be toxic because of the relentless pace and conflict. Leaders jostle for power and influence. Invisible hierarchies lead to dynamics where individuals behave like critical parents and angry children. When the environment is like this, you expend your energy surviving not thriving.

There will be times when you will feel like Sisyphus in trying to move a situation forward and finding yourself back at square one. There is no doubt that being a leader in any of the five domains of leadership is hard work so you will need stamina. Your work ethic can help you manage heavy workloads, but every human being has limits. Beware if you are a perfectionist – this trait could derail your performance as you attempt always to achieve one hundred per cent.

Be aware that someone can replace you, if you are unable to do the work. Yes, it becomes more difficult if you have a specific area of expertise or if you have been with your employer for years and they want to retain your knowledge and networks. However, when economic times are hard, salary bills get cut and people leave. But remember that if someone else can do your work, then it is also achievable by you. If you can accept these facts then the challenges of your leadership role may feel less insurmountable.

In recent years, I have been amazed by how much talk there has been around wellbeing. We have had mental toughness seminars, happiness policies, resilience training, mindfulness apps, cognitive behavioural therapy to manage anxiety and so on. These are some of the tried and tested approaches for coping with the external forces that exert pressure in the five domains, but the pressure will also come from within you.

The nature of the five domains will not change except for becoming more intense. So to cope with the environment that is created, you will have to change and then maintain any changes.

Every leader I meet wants to perform well. Over the years, while talking with them, wherever they are in the world, a recurring topic is their busyness, their resulting energy deficit and their desire to find practical ways to replace it. Those who have figured this out run outside, call their families, climb hills, meditate, dance or listen to uplifting music. This keeps them charged so that they can continue doing their valuable work and stay productive.

One day you might unexpectedly buckle from the pressure of resource constraints, high expectations and stakeholder demands. It takes a reservoir of energy to lead and you will need a never-ending supply.

Take a moment to ponder on the following questions:

What energises you?
How often do you replenish your energy?

Without a strong connection to your energy sources you cannot sustain your contribution.

HAVING AMBITION

DANIELA'S STORY

She told me 'I want to shape the future not just respond to it.' Daniela had big dreams to improve healthcare facilities for migrant mothers in the Middle East and The Leader's Call *was getting louder. Having run a successful business for thirty years and been a community volunteer, she felt that she was under no illusion about what it would take to see her desires become a reality.*

Developing innovative products, attracting new business, leading a team and delivering projects were her strengths. She was seen by others as being a role model and the seminars that she gave at the local chamber of commerce were always well attended. She had lots of 'connections', 'followers' and 'friends' across her social media platforms.

When we met, Daniela had almost given up hope because she could not see a practical way of turning her intention into something measurable and tangible. Despite a strong feeling that her strengths were needed, her zeal turned to frustration. Though Daniela had the commitment, competence and confidence to match her vision, as we talked, I sensed that she was trying to achieve this ambition the same way that she ran a business.

I shared my thoughts and at first Daniela looked surprised. Then, unexpectedly, she became defensive, telling me she was not sure that was the case, saying that she was ready to do whatever it took and believed that she could. We agreed to disagree and Daniela told me she wanted to spend more time thinking over the ideas and plans that she had in her head and on paper.

Months later I had an email. Daniela explained that she had indeed been trying to fulfil this ambition in a way that was familiar and comfortable. She had assumed that she could do what she had always done. Now she realised this approach was not getting her anywhere and she had decided to start again. Instead of assuming that she knew exactly what to do, she asked herself one question: 'How can this ambition become a reality?'

To go fast go alone, to go far go together[1]

While mulling over the question, Daniela was given the biography of a leader whom she saw as a role model. As she read it, she started to understand what it might take for her to realise this ambition to see change in her country. This leader's book became her workbook as she made copious notes in the margins.

She reached the conclusion that to make her dream come true she would need to focus on this single problem of improving healthcare provision for mothers. She also needed to connect with a large and diverse group of people who shared her concerns, her values and a desire to see change.

[1]African proverb

Inspired by the story of her role model, she posted a question across her social media networks. In days she had a flurry of interest. This flurry turned into an online forum where opinions, knowledge and ideas were shared. The forum became a small group of collaborators who were also committed to seeing the change happen in her country. Some had been born there, others had travelled there and others were simply curious.

This small group of collaborators agreed to start an online campaign. If they could find more people of like heart and mind then this critical mass might realise the ambition. The online campaign was a huge success attracting political leaders, journalists, institutions, local people and leaders who all shared Daniela's mission. A small group had turned into a global movement who all had a vested interest in seeing the ambition come to pass.

Later that year we met for lunch and I was so excited to hear about what had happened since our conversation months earlier. Daniela told me 'I learnt that while I had a lot to offer and do myself, I needed others to come and share the ambition. Not only that, but to expand it, challenge it and co-create it. My strengths and experience were not enough. But I believe that our collective voice is making the difference that I have been dreaming of.'

Daniela had a big dream to do something meaningful. Changing her country was not an ego trip, it was about how to help others prosper. She knew the problems that needed solutions. She also knew that the solutions would have to be simple, replicable and work at scale. Daniela could do a lot but she could not do everything. The daunting task was only achievable as she stood alongside others. The result was Daniela went to and stayed at the next level.

Collaborate to achieve your ambitions

Would you like to lead a BIG cause which is in the service of others? If so, then you will most certainly need to connect with a diverse network of stakeholders, perhaps in unlikely places, who will cooperate. I love Margaret Mead's quote: 'Never doubt that a small group of thoughtful, committed citizens can change the world; indeed, it's the only thing that ever has.'

Daniela sought out and found that small group. I too am blessed to have worked with ambitious people and organisations during my leadership experiences. I find their strong will and desire to carve a unique niche in the future inspiring, motivating and fulfilling, especially when it is aligned with seeking to make the world a better place.

What is your deepest desire? What is tugging at your heart strings or stirring your soul?

What conversations are you constantly having in your head? What in the world excites, frustrates or saddens you? What aspirations are you putting off?

Are you telling yourself that you cannot achieve the dream because it is too big? Who among your family and friends lovingly tell you to 'just do it' and offer to help?

Realising your ambition always starts with a choice. Think about who you need to work with in order to make your ambition a reality.

KEEPING PERSPECTIVE

PAJ'S STORY

'I can't see the wood for the trees. Each day I am bombarded with emails and I dash from meeting to meeting. My key stakeholders interrupt me when they like; I am expected to make decisions and resolve crises that arise. On top of all that I have an under-resourced team!' Paj was exasperated and very close to 'losing it'. It was not difficult to understand why: the environment created by the five domains was simply too immense.

Paj was doing a job that she had created in an organisation, which was close to her heart. Her usual calm demeanour had turned into irritability. She complained of lacking the clarity she needed to be able to fulfil the organisation's ambitious growth plans. Paj did not want to give up or run away from her role and responsibilities, but she did not want to continue like this either. 'It sounds as if you've lost perspective,' I said emphatically. Paj agreed 'You've hit the nail on the head; but how do I get it back?'

For Paj, perspective was about staying connected to why she had taken on the role – this is where her motivation came from. Her desire was always to create value for those she worked with and for. This was an anchor that kept her grounded but she had lost sight of it due to the daily 'firefighting' of issues, of decision making and of busyness!

Perspective was also about her ability to step back from the nitty gritty of operational detail, take in the bigger picture and stay on track. She had become side-tracked by the pressure and demands. This led to stress, under which Paj was unable to connect with what was most important *or see it clearly. Instead she focused on details and micro-managed her team, most of whom were capable of getting on and doing what was needed.*

Be careful what you wish for

Paj came to see me as a last resort. In her prior roles she had welcomed autonomy, with ad hoc support from her line manager, team and peers. However, since she had taken on this new role of leading the innovation department, which she persuaded her employer to let her create, Paj had become a 'victim' of her own success and she was floundering.

On inheriting departments in the past she was used to picking up the baton and settling down in the role within three months. This track record had given her a reputation for trouble-shooting and turning failing departments and teams around. Having done this many times Paj was bored. She was also aware that a common issue in all the departments she had led was a lack of ability to innovate.

When we met, Paj brought a list of the main issues she faced: leading a new department, too many emails, meetings and decisions, micro-managing stakeholders and team management. A moment of clarity came during our conversation. Paj had underestimated how different this role was to the others. In the past she was improving what she had inherited, now she was starting a department from scratch and with the steep learning curve she had lost confidence. She told me that she appreciated the safe non-judgemental space we had co-created for her to be more objective about her daily leadership situations and experiences.

Her prior leadership experiences had refined her skills in prioritising, communicating, negotiation, change management, setting boundaries and delegating. Paj realised she had the techniques to stay focused, take control, influence others and deliver the outcomes.

As we worked together it became clear to me that Paj valued having a sounding board and a regular space where she could reflect on her practice as a leader. Fortunately, she had a supportive line manager, good relationships with her peers and a team that respected and trusted her. They all brought different perspectives to the job in hand and she sought them out. Her only frustration was that they also struggled to see the wood and the trees!

Nearing the end of her mentoring programme, Paj decided that having regular time away for structured, strategic reflection was essential. At first she could not grasp how her absence would enhance her overall performance. She thought that this time could be used to complete tasks on her to-do list. Paradoxically, these 'perspective sessions' sustained her contribution; while seeking clarity she became more focused, motivated and her confidence returned. Perspective enabled her to become a more effective leader.

She told me what she valued most was being able to look at situations from different angles. She had become so used to seeing things in one or two dimensions, as if looking at only the front and back of an object. Our sessions had given her the ability to see the object from the inside and outside, top and bottom, on the side and the edges. Paj said 'I now have a bird's eye view as well as a view that is close to the ground. I can see so much more.'

Paj learnt how to challenge her assumptions. As her frame of reference changed she saw the challenges and opportunities of this new role from numerous standpoints. This gave her a better sense of proportion and more patience! She no longer accepted that her perception and interpretation of events was the 'only' reality. The greater her perspective, the better placed she was to grasp what was really going on and what needed to be done.

Seeing the whole picture

If I invited one hundred leaders to join me in a conversation about leadership, most if not all would relate to Paj and her story.

This daily experience is replicated across all sectors, industries and continents whatever the leader's age, culture or gender. Leaders often ask me if this experience is unique to them, their teams and organisations. When I tell them not completely, they are relieved to know they are not alone and yet at the same time they are exasperated. 'How are we supposed to lead effectively with all this going on?' they ask. 'This is the challenge and the opportunity of the next level,' I reply.

There is so much to do at the next level that it is easy just to keep your head down and never look up or step back from where you are. There may have been a time when keeping your head down and getting things done was rewarded. As you move from one level to another you will, however, need to be able to stand back regularly, just as Paj learned to do.

As you embrace new leadership experiences, your ability to be strategic, not just operational, will be needed.

Being strategic is a skill that leaders are told is necessary if they want to progress up or along the organisation hierarchy. It is a difficult skill to develop if you are in a role that maximises your operational and technical skills. You may have to go outside your place of work to find opportunities that develop this strategic ability.

By now you will be clear that *The Leader's Call* takes you out of your comfort zone into what is called the 'stretch zone'. Beyond that is the 'panic zone'. Many leaders find themselves there – often! It is not unusual, it is not their fault, it just happens. I have found that perspective is what helps me to move back from panic to stretch and stay there for longer.

Why is perspective so important? We know that it means how we see, for example, a situation, an experience or an interaction that is past, present or coming up. But do not be tricked into thinking that perspective is just about what we see or do not see. When done best it is multi-sensory. While leading we must learn to pay attention to what we feel, think, hear and sense. In practice this means taking a more holistic approach when trying to understand what is really going on around and inside us.

Paj's story illustrates the importance of being able to see more clearly when a 'blizzard' of tasks, expectations and demands are coming at you, whichever way you turn. Of course, you can make your way forward in a blizzard with your eyes scrunched together and half closed but it is risky, and if others are following you they are at risk too. Much better to find a safe space away from the blizzard where you can gather yourself.

If she had known that one hundred leaders felt the

same as her, Paj's exasperation would have been less. Such knowledge could have had a 'normalising' effect resulting in her feeling comforted by the reality that she was not alone. When leaders get together and feel safe in each other's company I have observed time and time again how perspectives are shared, challenged and embraced. Leaders need more safe, non-judgemental spaces where they can meet, take stock, be challenged, listen, stay grounded and contribute.

Ignorance is not bliss

Leaders can be hugely successful in making a difference and I celebrate this. However, remember that we all have flaws in our character. We make assumptions, have blind spots, an Achilles' heel, unconscious bias, ingrained attitudes and we project our shadow self. We overplay strengths, succumb to group-think and wilful blindness. We form cliques, dysfunctional relationships and toxic cultures. When leaders resist different points of view and are self-reliant they will derail themselves and others who are with them.

Perspective reveals underlying causes, hidden tensions and stuck mind sets. It can nudge leaders away from unhelpful behavioural habits and immoral conduct. In practice, leaders need to surround themselves with all kinds of people, for example through joining different networks – exposure to a diverse range of opinions and feedback can reap benefits. Leaders become more ethical, accountable, innovative, make better decisions, have fewer errors of judgement and lead credibly with integrity. All this will enable you, as a leader, to sustain your contribution and leave a lasting legacy.

PRACTISING GENEROSITY

TOBI'S STORY

He was a very experienced leader whose retirement was on the horizon. Tobi did not want it to 'creep up on him', he wanted to maintain his zest for life and explore how he could be of use to others. He knew that I had coached several leaders in his network who were nearing retirement. They finished the programme with greater clarity than when they had started. Some had taken action and were intentionally practising generosity each week.

Tobi was not keen on the idea of legacy; he thought it was a self-inflated notion. 'Legacy is for people who are doing big things in the world. I'm doing my little thing where I am.' Instead, 'giving back' was how Tobi described what he wanted to do. He was keen to become involved in his local community and instinctively felt that with his years of experience in different leadership roles, he had something to offer; he was just not sure what.

After our first session he decided to look at his local council website and peruse the A to Z list of services being delivered by the borough and local groups. He used this as a checklist to identify what resonated with him most strongly and where he might volunteer. There were crosses against the services that had no appeal, question marks against those he was not sure about and ticks against those with which he felt a genuine connection.

With a few months of free weekends coming up, Tobi decided to take a closer look at the community services with question marks and ticks beside them. Being employed on a part-time basis and running his own business meant that Tobi had the flexibility to visit during the week those that did not operate at the weekend.

What Tobi really enjoyed most of all during this ground research was meeting those working in these services and the people who benefited from them. He found it easy to talk to them and listen to their stories of trial and triumph. On several occasions he was moved to tears and his desire to be of use grew. He was surprised at the generosity of the service workers, the majority of whom were volunteers who freely gave their time and skills to support those who were in need.

Tobi felt overwhelmed by the number of services where he could give back – the needs in his local community were so great. As he reflected on the conversations, he narrowed his list based on where he had had the greatest emotional connection with those he had met. He suspected it was there where he could make a lasting contribution.

Following his retirement Tobi emailed me to share his news. He had become chair of a homeless charity, mentor for a children's project and fundraiser for a regeneration and growth initiative. He was putting his instinctive leadership abilities and his network of contacts to use. At times he was busier than when he had worked but he loved it!

Acts of service

If you think that legacy is by its very nature generous, you are correct. While a legacy can be left accidentally, our focus here is on sustaining your contribution intentionally to benefit those with whom you are working and helping now, as well as those who will come after you. It is also about making sure you are focused on legacy for its own sake rather than trying to get noticed or satisfy your ego!

Your community needs you to make it a better place! There are individuals, families, teams, groups, districts, organisations and institutions looking for a leader like you. Whether you are addressing symptoms or underlying issues your involvement will generate both small and sizeable shifts. Over time, deeper societal change occurs because every small shift adds up to create seismic change.

Many of us take for granted what we have, what we acquire and what is given to us. I have met a countless number of generous leaders. These leaders are giving back to others while they are alive through random and planned acts of service where they reside and work and in the places they travel to and visit around the world. The most precious thing you can offer others, apart from your commitment, uniqueness and abilities, is your time.

Whether you are listening, agitating, cooking, planning, writing, visiting, cleaning, mentoring, fundraising, running, campaigning, supporting or organising, all of these and more are the acts of service that have a potential to create a wonderful environment in the five domains of leadership. Know that your generosity will multiply as it is passed on even if you do not see it. When these acts come back to you in the same or another form receive them with gratitude to encourage the giver and to keep the cycle of altruism and philanthropy going.

True generosity is giving consistently with the intention to do good without a hidden agenda or strings attached. It is giving without the expectation that the receiver will return that act; but do not be surprised when you receive positive benefits too. It is hoping that whatever is given will be used well and to optimum effect. To be generous is to extend your heart and soul to unlock and release the giving potential of others.

WHAT KEEPS ME GOING

I have taken part in the development and growth of thousands of global leaders which has given me immense pleasure. This has been made possible through the many next levels I have moved to, the multiple roles that came with these and the areas where I honed and expanded my expertise. From customer service to human resources, organisational learning to leadership development and from talent management to running a niche business.

Over the past twenty something years of doing this work I have discovered – through trial and error, regret and success – a mix of things that works for me as I seek to be my best, to sustain my contribution, make a mark and leave a legacy behind. Here are examples of how I stay energised and sustain my contribution.

SOURCING ENERGY
- **Quality time with family and friends**
- **One-day retreats every three months**
- **Supporting community philanthropy**

HAVING AMBITION
- **Writing down and sharing my learning**
- **Joining global leadership networks**
- **Collaborating with diverse partners**

KEEPING PERSPECTIVE

- Journaling to review my behaviour
- Support circles of mentors and peers
- Creative trips to see and try new things

PRACTISING GENEROSITY

- Mentoring the next generation of leaders
- Connecting leaders to those in my network
- Pro bono work in the UK and Africa

Doing these things means I am less likely to be set in my ways as I respond to the things that press my buttons or get under my skin. I experiment with solutions and stay up to date within my field of expertise. I have developed the emotional fortitude needed to respond to *The Leader's Call*, to thrive at the next level and succeed in the five domains of leadership. I hope that this book encourages, equips and enables you and the new breed of leaders who are trying to find and adopt different leadership styles.

What mix of things are you doing to keep yourself going so that you can keep sustaining your contribution?

PLAN YOUR LEGACY

Years ago I bought a magazine that documented the lives of historic leaders – men and women who shaped the world, transforming it and tainting it. It got me thinking about the leadership stories I might tell my grandchildren and young people who are developing their leadership skills. Stories about the challenges I faced and overcame. Stories about failure, success and the lessons learnt. You and I are creating a leadership legacy now.

We can speculate and imagine but none of us really knows how we will be remembered. All we can do is be good stewards of the inheritance that has been passed on to us professionally or personally. We can cherish and share the heritage left behind with the generation of leaders to come.

We have all stood on the shoulders of leaders to reach where we are and there are those who will stand on our shoulders to reach further than where we are. A friend told me a beautiful story about his grandfather, who planted trees for his children so that as they grew the trees would grow. Not only that but he planted trees for his grandchildren and the great grandchildren that were not yet born and whom he would never see.

How will you remember those leaders who have gone before you? How will you keep their spirit of excellence and endeavour alive? This is important because when we know about these leaders we are inspired to achieve more. We are multiplying their legacy.

For whom are you being a role model? What kind of leadership environment and experiences are you passing on and leaving behind for the generation of leaders you will never see? While you cannot determine the final outcome of your legacy, do not leave it to chance. St Gregory said that what is not consciously embraced cannot be transformed.

ACTIONS TO TAKE

Life is full of surprises and none of us know how much time we have left on planet Earth. I do not write this to scare you but rather to urge you to take responsibility for your life and leadership experiences. Why have regrets if you can start doing something about what really matters today? If this chapter has provoked thoughts that you want to follow up or reminded you about something you want to leave behind, then take action.

On pages 165 to 166 I gave you twelve examples of what I am doing to stay energised, to be ambitious, to maintain perspective and to be generous. All these are how I sustain my contribution and ensure that while my legacy is being created I am being and doing my best.

What about you?

SOURCING ENERGY

1 ....

2 ....

3 ....

KEEPING PERSPECTIVE

1 ....

2 ....

3 ....

HAVING AMBITION

1 ....

2 ....

3 ....

PRACTISING GENEROSITY

1 ....

2 ....

3 ....

Being a leader means that while you are the agent for your contribution and legacy, you are also subject to restrictive constraints, growing pressure, competing demands and other factors beyond your control. However, you are also presented with incredible opportunities, surprising moments, unexpected blessings and the privilege of making positive change. Do what you can wherever you lead and let the value you create take care of itself.

The African Diaspora Kids legacy community project gives me lots of energy, especially when I see young people enjoying our activities. Since our launch in May 2015, we have held family fun days, visited historic places of interest, shared interesting facts and stories via our blog page and run several 'Introducing Africa' sessions in local schools.

I have grown hugely through this project. How? Being a novice community leader has exposed me to many models and approaches for community development which are new to me! I have engaged with a greater diversity of stakeholders, who each have their own needs and desires. What I have enjoyed most of all is reconnecting with my interest and passion for arts, culture and heritage. It means that I can express my creativity more and enable others to do the same!

I have been encouraged by the strangers I have met who are now friends and who share the same and complementary ambitions – we are now collaborators. This small group of volunteers are my sounding board when I fail to see the bigger picture and their generosity in giving back astounds me again and again. Together we are doing something for Ghana and for the beautiful continent of Africa.

IT IS YOUR MOVE

In this chapter, I have shared what I consider to be important aspects for sustaining your contribution. I have given you some examples from my personal and professional life. You have found out how other leaders have grappled with the situations and stresses you face.

Know that being a leader means that you are powerful even when you feel powerless. You can choose to stay where you are or go forward. My prayer is that you will not let anything or anyone (not even yourself) hold you back. The world needs your contribution and the next generation are waiting for your legacy. I hope that you feel more confident to make a move. The next level can be hard work but it is always worthwhile!

'Do your little bit of good where you are; it's those little bits of good put together that overwhelm the world'

Desmond Tutu

AND FINALLY...

> ### 'Nothing ventured, nothing gained'
> Benjamin Franklin

We are at the end of this book and you are moving on. I have imagined you as I wrote: picturing where you may have been, where you are and where *The Leader's Call* is taking you. Pause for a moment on this threshold.

How do you feel about where you are going next?

I hope my words can be the practical inspiration that you need during your leadership transition as you move into one of the five domains, where you can bring your commitment, your true self, a willingness to keep learning and a desire to create a legacy.

What you have read may appear to be common sense but it is not always common practice. From a distance being a leader appears to be straightforward but up close (and when it is personal) it is very complex. My vision is to equip you, the leader, to make a greater positive impact because when you do the ripple effect of the benefits are felt near and far in the five domains and for years, even centuries to come.

This book is the leadership development programme I have wanted for my next levels but never had, until now.

It has also been a much needed opportunity for me to reflect on and consolidate what I have learned as a leader and what leaders have taught me.

You can use it in future as a trusty guide to assess where you have been, where you are now and where you are going. I know that you can and will do awesome things in the five domains of leadership!

Here is a quick reminder of what we covered in the four insights.

- **Insight one – Commitment:** non commitment, over commitment, start stop commitment, ongoing commitment
- **Insight two – Authenticity:** knowing yourself, being true to yourself, expressing yourself, accepting yourself
- **Insight three – Learning:** leadership experience, transferable skills, seeking knowledge, continuous development
- **Insight four – Legacy:** sourcing energy, having ambition, keeping perspective and practising generosity

You may want to re-read the sections that are most pertinent to you now. Second readings and subsequent ones will reinforce these insights and reveal your own.

When I first heard *The Leader's Call* in Ghana, West Africa on a new road with its gleaming tarmac and clear road markings I did not know where I was going, but it has been an incredible adventure. It has taken me down roads that were well worn, bumpy with potholes and strewn with danger signs. Others were under construction and in order to continue on my way I have had to take a detour, but I have always managed to get back on track.

All these roads have taken me to interesting places and spaces within and outside myself. I would not change a thing because I have become so much richer for it all and now I am a better 'driver'! Most of all, these adventures are what have revealed more of who I truly am and shaped the authentic leader I am today.

I hope, above all, that you will take away two things from this book.

You are a leader

Being a leader is not for the elite or the few who have been 'chosen'. *The Leader's Call* is an invitation to all those who are willing to respond, to follow the trail of clues courageously and boldly step up to the next level.

You lead yourself

Always remember that you do not have to squeeze yourself into any social, cultural, gender, sector or industry moulds. Now, more than ever, leadership is about being real and comfortable in your own skin. No one else does exactly what you do in exactly the way you do it. And no one ever will!

'To learn to fly, a bird must leave the nest'
African proverb

GO-TO RESOURCES FOR LEADERS

There are so many resources out there and I encourage you to seek out those that work for you. Here are just a few that I can personally recommend.

Insight 1: C is for Commitment
Moving to the next level

Career Leader – I used this to pinpoint the field where I wanted to be a leader **www.careerleader.com**

Street Wisdom – I love the idea that wisdom is all around you: just take a look! **www.streetwisdom.org**

Third Sector, Haymarket Media Group. This magazine and website are an informative read if you want to know about the charitable world **www.thirdsector.co.uk** and **www.haymarket. com/brands/third-sector**

Insight 2: A is for Authenticity
Becoming who you are

Blob Tree – a resource for 'simple' pictures to help raise your self-awareness **www.blobtree.com**

House of Colour – discover your signature colours, personal style and image with a multiple award-winning consultant such as Fiona Ingham **www.houseofcolour.co.uk/find-a-stylist/ profile/62**

People Management, Haymarket Media Group for Chartered Institute of Personnel and Development. This magazine is my staple for keeping up to date with all things people-related in the workplace **www.cipd.co.uk/pm** and **www.haymarket.com/ brands/people-management**

Insight 3: L is for Learning
Developing mastery

Center for Creative Leadership – to be a creative leader take a look at this website **www.ccl.org/leadership**

TED – an online global community that needs no introduction! Be inspired by new ideas from leaders round the globe **www.ted.com**

Learning at Work Week – an annual event led by Campaign for Learning that is a great way to promote learning while working

www.campaign-for-learning.org.uk/cfl/learningatworkweek

Insight 4: L is for Legacy
Sustaining your contribution

Reflective Practice – Writing and Professional Development, Dr Gillie Bolton, Sage Publications Ltd, 2014. This book showed me how to extract learning from my leadership experiences. It is brilliant and challenging

If being a leader gets too much the British Association for Counselling and Psychotherapy and the Stress Management Society will equip you to find coping strategies so that you can thrive not just survive **www.bacp.co.uk** and **www.stress.org.uk**

The Good Retreat Guide – 6th edition, Stafford Whiteaker, Hay House UK, 2010. Find a spiritual oasis wherever you are in the world and keep going back to it!

ABOUT THE AUTHOR

Grace Owen is a leadership development consultant. For over twenty years she has developed thousands of leaders from around the world, at non-executive, board, senior, middle, junior and graduate levels, to excel and make a greater impact wherever they are. This work has taken her across the continent of Africa and into world-class organisations such as the Chartered Institute of Personnel and Development, UNICEF UK, Camfed International, Bromley by Bow Centre, London Business School, the BBC, Brit Insurance, the NHS, Lloyds Bank, Barclays Bank, Marks & Spencer and Costa Coffee.

Grace was featured in *Third Sector* magazine online, BBC online, *The Bookseller*, Fresh Business Thinking, *The Guardian*, *Metro*, Reconnect Africa, *Pride* magazine, *Stylist* magazine, TNT jobs, *The Times* and *Career Developments*. She has been a guest speaker for radio and podcasts. Her first book *The Career Itch – 4 Steps for Taking Control of What You Do Next* was published in 2009.

Working with Grace

To discuss bespoke leadership development needs for you, your group, team, organisation or institution please get in touch with Grace at **www.grace-owen.com**